# Toughest Job
# in Britain

# JEREMY SPAKE
# Toughest Job in Britain

B⬚XTREE

*This book is dedicated to my dear friends*
*Nick, Kyra and, of course, Tarzan the lamb*

First published 2002 by Boxtree
an imprint of Pan Macmillan Ltd
Pan Macmillan, 20 New Wharf Road, London N1 9RR
Basingstoke and Oxford
Associated companies throughout the world
www.panmacmillan.com

ISBN 0 7522 2008 X

By arrangement with the BBC

The BBC logo and Toughest Job in Britain are word marks
and trademarks of the British Broadcasting Corporation
and are used under licence.
BBC logo © BBC 1996
Toughest Job in Britain © BBC 2001

9 8 7 6 5 4 3 2

A CIP catalogue record for this book is available from
the British Library.

Typeset by seagulls
Printed and bound in Great Britain by Mackays of Chatham plc, Kent

# contents

# acknowledgements

This is my favourite part of any book, because this is the bit where the author gets the chance to go wild and have a good old ramble through the list of people who have contributed to its pages. As you might expect, I'm going to be no exception to the rule, and for the next few pages will probably ramble on incoherently about the great and the good who have helped me, over the past few years, to achieve this interesting little read that is *Toughest Job in Britain*.

Where can I possibly begin to thank people? Well, I guess the most logical place is with the wonderful men and women who allowed my crew and me to invade their lives to film their Tough Jobs. Not all of them are mentioned in this book, because there wasn't enough space to write about every job we filmed. However, each of you is a star in your own right, for tackling one of the most unbelievable jobs in the land. You're a real credit to yourselves, and I feel honoured to have shared a few days with you, even if I wasn't a lot of help!

I'd also like to thank all the businesses and organizations who helped smooth away the red tape before we started filming, including Abbas Cabins, Blackpool Tower, Greater Manchester Ambulance Service Trust, The Jay Miller Circus and Thames Water, to name but a very few.

Big thanks to Emma Marriott, of Boxtree, Pan Macmillan, for commissioning this book, and to Katy Carrington, who pored over every page of my tome, editing them with Hazel Orme's help. In fact the entire team at Boxtree have all our gratitude for making the book a reality – cheers, folks!

No word of thanks could be complete unless I mention my family, who sat and listened to every word even when they didn't want to. Thanks, folks, once again you've aided my struggle to complete a book. Without you all, I probably wouldn't have finished it in time.

Now if all that wasn't enough, I need to thank as many of the BBC team as possible. While not everyone from the team is mentioned in the book, they all played a vital role in making the series, and I would like to thank each of them.

Executive producers, who were charged with taking overall control of the series production.

| | |
|---|---|
| Series One | Nick Vaughan-Barratt |
| Series Two | Vicki Barrass |

Series producers, who had the unenviable task of dealing with the day-to-day production nightmares.

| | |
|---|---|
| Series One | Gary Hunter |
| Series Two | Juliet Rice |

Directors, who struggled through thick and thin on location to help make the filming run smoothly.

| | |
|---|---|
| Series One | Gary Hunter |
| | Barbie Maclauren |
| | John Maguire |
| | Sally Norris |
| Series Two | Nicola Jinks |
| | Mike Montgomery |

Researchers, without whom none of the stories would have been found. I also owe them thanks for keeping us fed and watered during the long hours spent filming.

| | |
|---|---|
| Series One | Leceia Gordon |
| | Mary Biles |
| | Julie Soper |
| Series Two | Natalie Watts |
| | Alison Hollies |
| | Rhys Pritchard |

Production managers, who should really have featured in the series themselves (trying to manage the series budget is a nightmare). Thanks also for making sure the teams and I were safe on location.

| | |
|---|---|
| Series One | Craig Dancy |
| Series Two | Sarah Smith/Julia Smith |

Production secretaries, who do most of the running around for the production managers. Unsung heroes one and all.

| | |
|---|---|
| Series One | Zoë Taylor |
| Series Two | Emily Chapple |

Series cameramen, without whom I would have regularly gone insane.

| | |
|---|---|
| Series One | Denis Borrow |
| Series Two | Simon Priestman |

Camera assistant, who was run ragged trying to keep up with Denis.

| | |
|---|---|
| Series One | Stuart Brown |

Series sound recordists, thanks for listening to my dulcet tones throughout, you above all others deserve an award!

| | |
|---|---|
| Series One | Paul Paragon |
| Series Two | Guy Linton |

A whole load of thanks goes to all other crew members, including Dominic and Bridget who directed a couple of the films, Mike Carling and Brian his sound engineer, for braving the heat of Oman; Vaughan, a great Kiwi cameraman, and Andrew, the perpetually hungry sound engineer, for their efforts on behalf of the series and, of course, the folks at Clear Cut Pictures in Shepherds Bush, who had to edit every last minute of our work into the finished series. Not an easy task, I can assure you.

Finally – I did warn you this would go on a bit, did I not? – Peter Salmon, the former BBC One controller, for commissioning the series in the first place, and to Lorraine Heggessey, his successor, who wanted to see a second series of *Toughest Job in Britain*.

Thank you, one and all!

# introduction

**W**hy is it that most of us are only ever wise after the event and not before it? Strange that... if I'd cottoned on sooner to what the BBC had in mind when I accepted the challenge to present a new series called *Toughest Job in Britain*, I might not have been writing this now! The experience has definitely been one of those 'where fools rush in' moments in a person's life and you're about to discover why.

It all started in 1998 when Nick Vaughan-Barratt and Vicki Barrass, both producers at the BBC, were tasked with the job of developing a series for me to present. We had several essential lunch-time meetings, as you do, where we managed to sample the odd glass of wine whilst trying to come up with a range ideas for the BBC One controller to consider commissioning. After much discussion about the type of things that interest me, such as international espionage (for some reason they weren't too keen on my idea of travelling around the former Soviet Union seeking out retired and not-so-retired spies – can't think why. I still think it would have made a brilliant series), we agreed that we should try to find an idea that would enable me to meet as many members of the general public as possible. I can only imagine that my former career at Heathrow airport with Aeroflot Russian International Airlines had given Nick and his team the inspiration for the show. After all, when you've dealt with losing the Moscow Philharmonic Orchestra, a pregnant mum at check-in and a flat aircraft tyre in an average shift at Heathrow, almost any other career might seem tame by comparison.

Several silent months went by before Nick, who has always been supportive of my media career, invited me into the BBC's offices in Wood Lane, London, to discuss the final selection of ideas. 'Jeremy, we've narrowed it down to one concept, which we think you're going to love. We'd like you to go off in search of the person who has the "Toughest Job in Britain"!' exclaimed Nick, and a new series was born. What follows are my personal experiences and recollections of just a handful of the thirty-eight truly memorable jobs we have filmed for both the first and second series of this challenging programme. Those jobs that didn't make it into the book are no less worthy of inclusion than those that did. I simply ran out of space and was forced to choose a cross-section of those that encapsulated the essence of my search.

As you might expect from a search of this nature, there has to be an overall winner. Now, I can hear you say, how do you decide what is tough? That's a good question, and not one that's all that easy to answer. Do the hours make a job tough? The boss? The working conditions? Maybe the rate of pay, or a combination of any of the above. As you can see, many factors come into play, so to make life a bit easier for me to decide - and yes, it did have to be my choice - the production team and I decided to introduce an overall mark for how tough a particular job can be. Rather logically, we called this a 'Toughness Rating'. Okay, maybe it's not that inventive but it sums it up beautifully, don't you think? The rating is made up of three categories:

1: Stress
2: Danger
3: Yuck Factor

We decided that each category would be worth a maximum of 5 points, thus giving a total overall 'Toughness Rating' out of 15. As you delve deeper into the murky world of unpleasant occupations you'll discover the points each job earned. For those that featured in the first series and weren't given a rating because we hadn't come up with such an inventive way of making the all-important decision, I've added one retrospectively so that you can gauge all of the jobs equally. If you're now feeling a tad confused, panic not: as you read on all will become clear.

Throughout my quest to discover who has it toughest, I have been reminded of my first visit to a school's resident careers adviser nearly twenty years ago. Was it *really* that long ago? Frightening! It was a particularly unpleasant experience, as I remember, which saw me arguing with a fairly elderly chap who had a distracting spot on his nose, about why I wanted to work at Heathrow airport. He seemed hell bent on persuading me to give up my foolish desires. 'Don't be ridiculous, Spake! Heathrow is over a hundred miles away, and you have no airline experience. You'll never get a job there!' is my somewhat hazy memory of his advice. Boy, am I glad I ignored him (I wonder if he saw *Airport*?). Although I had a bit of a struggle on my hands, I eventually got a job at the airport, and enjoyed every minute of my time there. I never thought, though, that I'd find myself presenting a series about jobs and end up feeling a bit like the dear old careers adviser chap. I've spent many an hour trying to dissuade the truly great people who featured in both series of the show from doing the jobs they have. From Maggie Barton, a truly remarkable woman who, with her husband, works eighteen hours a day managing a fish merchant's business in Billingsgate Market, London, to Kenny Young, who has dedicated his working career to keeping London's sewers clear of muck, I have repeatedly failed to convince my worthy contributors that they should visit the job centre. In fact, one thing that is true about all of the people who have participated in filming, is their overwhelming commitment to the task in hand, which they perform without so much as a moan. As scary as it may seem, as you read on, most of them had a smile on their face to boot!

Before you launch yourself into my utterings, I feel that a small word of warning is needed. If, like me, you are occasionally work-shy, especially when physical labour is mentioned, now might be a good time to put this book down, just in case the contents bring you out in a cold sweat. Fear can be a terrible thing. But hang on, though! Make yourself comfortable because, actually you should read on! There's just a chance that you'll realize, as I did, that there are many unsung heroes among the working population of Britain who, despite the difficulties, just get on with it, allowing those of us unwilling to endure toughness to enjoy gentler pursuits in a bid to earn a living. If, however, you're one of those people who has it tough at work, and you've managed to escape our gaze while we were researching for the series, I hope you can find comfort in the knowledge that you're most definitely not alone. In fact, there is a whole bunch of you out there who are worthy contenders for the title 'Toughest Job in Britain'.

# chapter one
# SEWER-FLUSHER

***Salary:*** £15,000 average per annum

***Requirements:*** Applicants should be prepared to work round the clock, and be capable of working unsupervised in confined spaces. In addition, a cast-iron stomach and no sense of smell are essential.

***Toughness rating:*** 13

'**B**ut, Jeremy, come on, no serious search for Britain's Toughest Job would be complete without a visit to the sewers!' were the compelling words of Nick, the series' executive producer. Now, at this stage, you might not appreciate that he and I had sat and chatted six months earlier about those jobs I had no desire to investigate on behalf of the Great British Audience. And, yes, you guessed it, Sewer-Flusher was top of a very short list of just two jobs. What was the other job? Snake handler. No, thank you very much! Be fair, folks, we all have a phobia about something.

As much as it grieves me to do so, it's time to relive the nightmare that was the sewers of London. By now you've probably cottoned on to the fact that I wasn't keen to visit the bowels of the capital. After all, we can all imagine just how unpleasant it is down there, can't we? Wrong! You have no idea – believe me!

It was a cold, damp April day when I pulled up at the Thames Water depot in Hammersmith, which is home to the thirty-nine men who make up the flushing teams responsible for looking after London's network of 45–50 miles of stinking pipes and tunnels. All I'd been told was that I was to find Kenny Young, who would brief me on my duties for the day.

As I entered the depot, Gary, the film director, met me looking rather fetching in an enormous pair of hobnailed waders (extra-long welly-boots to you and me) and some white disposable overalls – you know the sort of thing I mean: you often see scene-of-crime police officers wearing them when they are investigating a major incident. Now, it's important for you to remember that I didn't want to be there, and that I needed to convince Gary that I really did want to become a sewer-flusher for the day.

'Morning, Gary, have you made contact with Kenny yet?' I asked, in a less-than-enthusiastic tone.

'Morning – he's not here yet,' came the reply, in a broad Scottish accent.

'Oh, shame, perhaps he's ill? Maybe he's not coming in today. Oh, what a pity, no, really, that's a shame. Are there any pubs round here that serve breakfast?'

Gary told me to join the rest of the film crew in the changing rooms, where he assured me that Kenny would meet us.

Damn! I'd already conjured up a bacon sandwich in my head.

As I entered the building I thought I'd better find out if anyone was about. 'Hello! Hello! is there anybody here?' I whispered. I didn't want anyone hearing me. However, no sooner had I tiptoed down the corridor, pretending not to be there, than a door creaked open and, yes, there was Kenny. Great! Marvellous!

'Come on, boy, we ain't got time to waste. Pop on those blue overalls [thankfully not the disposable variety], waders and harness and we'll get under way.' 'Cheers, Kenny, you're a real mate,' was my sombre response.

Kenny, whose face is crimson, is a well-built, jovial man. Let's face it, you need a sense of humour to work down the sewers, and he has spent more than twenty years under London. It's all in a day's work for him, which was why he'd ducked out of the room before I'd had a chance to ask where my breathing apparatus was. I had, though, been given a small silver tin to attach to my belt, which I was assured was all I would need in an emergency. Inside the tin I discovered a strong plastic bag with a tube attachment – it reminded me a bit of the life-jacket you find in an aircraft with the tube you blow into to inflate it. If anything happens down below you breathe into this bag and move as quickly as possible.

Leaving behind the comfort of the warm depot, I boarded a lorry, which had a compartment at the back for the crew to relax in, where I met the rest of the guys working on Kenny's team. 'Jeremy, meet the boys!'

Collectively the team of seven welcomed me. 'Wotcha, mate! Are you ready for this, then?'

'We hope you've got a strong stomach, the stench is right knockout!'

'Don't worry, though, lad, we'll make sure we scoop you out if you go for an unexpected poo-bath!' Laughter erupted, and it was clear that the flushers of London enjoyed a bit of banter. It struck me that being a flusher was all about camaraderie, and that you definitely needed to enjoy a laugh at other people's expense. There was a brief silence in the van as we confirmed where we were heading first, which left me wondering why I was doing this. And, more importantly, why these seemingly sane men were doing this day in, day out. I was going to have to spend the entire day with them to discover the answer.

All too quickly the lorry came to an abrupt halt at the end of Fulham Palace Road, and the men piled out towards the first of today's drain-hole covers. It had been explained to me that the team were carrying out a number of drain inspections to ascertain where blockage-clearance work should start. I discovered from Gary that, 'As the team carry out their drain inspections, they will attempt to clear any minor blockages with their shovels and picks. There's a good chance you'll be able to get stuck into some real graft. Sadly, we probably won't have time for anything major today so Kenny and his team will probably return later to clear any major problems we might discover during the day.'

With Gary's words in my head I urged the boys, 'Please don't lift the lid on that, guys, we haven't had a cuppa yet!' Yes, this was my pathetic attempt to stall the inevitable.

'Nah, the quicker we get ourselves down 'ere, the quicker we can come back up for a cup of splosh – unless, of course, you fancy drinking the water down 'ere.' Kenny gestured towards the now uncovered drain.

I hadn't been with him for more than half an hour, and it was already apparent that this man loved his chosen career. He spoke with some affection about his job, and when I asked, 'Why do you do this, Kenny?' he replied, 'I've done it all my life, ain't I? Course, it used to be better when we had two hundred blokes on the job, but it pays the bills.'

Was this the only thing that kept Kenny coming back for more every day?

'Basically, yeah! But the boys and I 'ave a good old laugh, we're a real bunch of jokers, us lot. And someone's gotta do this job, aint they?' As I glanced down the drain my face was obviously a picture to behold: the staff of an interior design shop were watching me, highly amused. The smile on their faces soon disappeared as the stench from the drains wafted towards the open shop door.

It was a good job we weren't back in sixteenth-century London: things were a lot worse when sewers were no more than cesspits overflowing into the gutters. King Henry VIII had decreed that everyone should be held responsible for keeping the stretch of sewer outside their homes clean. Then there were no teams of overall-clad flushers to save the public from such an unpleasant duty. Somehow I felt that the delicate flowers working inside the shop would have struggled to put on their rubber gloves, let alone launch themselves into the job of shifting this effluent.

The odour emanating from the hole was truly vile, disgusting and repugnant. If you've ever found yourself walking through the restaurant district of a large city on Bin Day, you'll begin to know what sort of aroma was charging up my nostrils. Imagine 10,000 rotting cabbages intermingled with decaying fruit and, of course, the inevitable human waste, and you may be starting to get a feel for just what it was like.

With considerable trepidation I stood at the edge of the abyss being hooked up to a safety line as the camera crew and Kenny went below. Paul, the sound recordist, was a top bloke and had invested in some tiger balm. According to him, if I placed copious amounts of it under my nose, the increasingly horrendous pong would disappear. Of course, watching me slap this stuff on like I was making a cheese-spread sandwich was a moment of great hilarity for the hardened team who did this job day in, day out. But I wasn't about to let their wisecracks put me off – oh, no way!

I was told to get into position at the top of the ladder, and wait for the usual cue, 'Action!', from Gary. Denis, cameraman *extraordinaire*, would then capture my first faltering steps into the deep. As I stood there I could relate to the fear that must have gone through the minds of the first men on the moon. This was definitely going to be one small step for mankind, and one enormous great leap into the doo-doo for Jeremy Spake.

'How are you doing down there, Den? Are you ready yet?' I yelled. I was getting impatient: my legs felt like lead weights. You ought to try standing in a pair of Herman Munster boots on a thin ladder for five minutes, see how you like it. The wait was getting too much, and I was just in the process of stepping back up to the street, when I lost my footing and ended up dangling on the safety line. Thankfully, two of the guys had taken my weight on the line and lifted me back to the street. 'Thanks, boys,' I sang, in true soprano style, the harness having split my difference in the fall. Needless to say, I was delighted to hear that Denis had missed all of this, and that there was no chance of my swinging exploits making it into one of those out-take programmes that are so popular on UK television.

'Action!' shouted Gary. Excuse me! Was he not aware that I had very nearly fallen twenty-five feet or so to the bottom of the first level of the sewer, and that I was now in a position to audition for Leslie Garrett's job? I put aside my discomfort in the groin area, and made my way carefully downwards. The moment had come.

'Oh, my God, it stinks!' was about all I could say as I descended a second ladder. Kenny greeted me at my first storm overflow, and told me to watch my step. Naturally, my first instinct was to look down. Big, big mistake. Ugh. It was horrible. The grated walkway leading towards the overflow tunnel was caked with a range of sanitary products, toilet paper, condoms and excrement. The tunnel itself was about ten feet high, and seemed to stretch into oblivion as I shone my torch along the sweeping shaft.

Now, you may be interested to learn at this point in my sorry tale that the first major underground sewer was constructed by British civil engineer Sir Joseph Bazalgette back in 1858 as a result of something called the 'Great Stink'. It was caused by huge quantities of raw sewage gathering in the river Thames, which forced thousands of people to flee the capital to avoid the pong. The word sewage, by the way, is an Old English word meaning 'seaward', and before the mid-nineteenth century the Thames was about the only place they could send seven million people's natural waste. Anyway, appointed by the Metropolitan Board of Works, Bazalgette had this grand scheme to construct 165 miles of main sewers, including a 1600-foot tunnel under the Thames through which to drain the capital's waste to the lower side of the river. The plan was approved and the tunnel, much to everyone's surprise, was built. It's reported that Queen Victoria was so impressed by this feat of engineering that she ordered a train line be put down there so that people could go and marvel at London's latest wonder. Believe it or not, the tunnel became a popular promenade and top tourist attraction, with people paying a small entrance fee to walk along its length. Today the tunnel is part of London Underground's Bakerloo Line.

Frankly, though, I'd have paid a king's ransom not to have been walking along the tunnel I was in! A further glance around my feet revealed whole pieces of fruit! Yes, fruit! Kenny told me then about a now retired colleague who used to pick up the whole pieces of fruit and eat them with his lunch! 'So, tell me, Kenny, what exactly do we need to do down here?' I asked, quickly, wanting to brush over the issue of eating what was floating by.

Before he answered, Kenny was eager for me to look to my right: 'There you go, boy, raw sewage heading for the treatment works.' I felt nauseous as the torch on top of my safety helmet shone down on an arterial sewage track. All manner of nasty things floated past like prizes on the *Generation Game* conveyor belt. All of this was being caught on film by Denis and Paul, who were now looking decidedly green around the gills. Gary, having been down with Kenny the week before, was already a past master at this.

Because there's a real risk of hydrogen sulphide, methane and lack of oxygen in the tunnel, one of the lads was attaching a special device to the side of a slime-encrusted ladder to monitor the level of dangerous gases. As he did so, he prodded Kenny to remind him to let me into a little secret – exactly what we were supposed to be doing down this positively vile hole.

'Well, the thing is all this muck 'ere causes blockages, and we need to clear it so that if there's a storm the sewer will not overflow into the street,' replied my smirking friend. 'This 'ere might look 'orrible to you, but just look at the engineering! Those Victorians certainly knew how to build tunnels. This is a marvel, and there ain't too many get the chance to 'ave a look down 'ere. We're all very privileged!' I wondered whether he knew that the Romans, with the Cretans, had led the act in sewer development. Having done a bit of reading up on the subject of sewage, I asked, 'Kenny, did you know Sir John Harington, back in 1589, created the first flushing WC for Queen Elizabeth I?'

Kenny smiled, 'Yeah, what about old Sir Thomas Crapper who tweaked Harington's earlier bog to make something very similar to the modern WC?' There was considerable laughter among the team, but my face was becoming more distorted by the minute as my nose battled with the stench. The tiger balm had failed in its mission to combat the onslaught of foul smells.

'Jeremy! Enough of all that, back to the job! This muck 'ere is too bad for us to be able to do anything much with it today. Job like this will take five men at least three weeks to clear.'

'Really, Kenny? Why so long?'

Still grinning from ear to ear, Kenny explained, 'We 'ave to come down 'ere with shovels and the like. There ain't no modern power tools that'll shift this rubbish, just good old elbow grease, as supplied by me and the boys.'

This seemed like an extraordinary way of working in today's modern world. I learned later that the men move systematically from sewer to sewer, generally working in teams of between five and eight with shovels and pickaxes. Routine inspections are carried out in each district of the capital, followed by scheduled blockage-clearance work. Naturally, this is a year-round task, which at times must feel like painting the Forth Bridge: no sooner do you reach the end than you have to start all over again. Routine work is only interrupted when a major unexpected blockage occurs that might have been missed during inspections. Some sewers have camera equipment to monitor waste levels at the depot.

Although I'd escaped the evil task of shovelling the muck, I was feeling really sick. Kenny and the boys weren't helping much as they were talking about the stench that results when they disturb the effluent and debris. 'Thing is, Jeremy, once you start moving this, it kicks up big time, and, of course, your face is right next to it while you're shovelling. Quality!'

I tried not to throw up all over the cameraman as I asked, 'What's next? Are we going back up top?'

Kenny ignored my question. 'Come on,' he said, 'we need to check that the water can still flow through if we leave it a week or so before starting the clear-up task.' My heart sank yet again as I looked towards the narrow corridor, festooned with hanging clods of mixed sewage. There was even a couple of wristwatches tangled up among the other delights.

Remember those boots? You know, the hobnailed Herman Munster waders? Well, they were a complete nightmare to walk in, and certainly not designed to complement the wet and slimy conditions underfoot. As I slipped and slid along I could feel the hanging debris dragging across my back. 'Kenny, is this a terrible health hazard down here?' I asked, hoping that my new boss was going to say, '*Not to worry, we'll go back to the ladders.*'

'Yeah, we have to have our jabs done regular, you know.'

Great.

After an hour and a half beneath Fulham Palace Road inspecting the tunnels, the novelty was wearing off. You won't be surprised to learn that I was over the moon to be told, 'OK, can't do no more 'ere, time for that brew, mate.' Music to my ears, and I was first up the ladders! I don't think the camera crew could quite believe their eyes – Jeremy being athletic? Surely not!

Emerging from the drain was an experience in itself: to see the public milling about then catching a whiff of what lay below was great fun. One old lady was most concerned that I'd hit hard times and had left Heathrow Airport to work in the sewers. It took me fifteen minutes to put her mind at rest that I was filming a series about the *Toughest Job in Britain*, and not working full-time as a flusher. 'Would you like to do this for a living, my love?' seemed like a reasonable thing to ask Doris, my new-found pensioner friend.

'Oh, no, love, no, definitely not. Come home ponging like that?' was Doris's profound response. It struck me then that Kenny and his colleagues up and down the country belong to a special breed: not many would rush to do this for a living.

After cleaning the gunk off my boots – *smmmmelly* – I stepped into the lorry for a well-earned cup of coffee. No sooner had my bum hit the less-than-comfortable seat than we were off to our next job. 'You're having a laugh, you lot! Where are we going now?' I asked, hoping they'd say the pub.

In unison, they replied, 'The Embankment, where we've got a very, very special job for you, boy!'

At this point I didn't know whether to laugh or cry as my mind ran amok with images of what might be next for me to behold.

As we trundled through the usual London traffic snarl-ups, the boys started to regale me with the sort of stories you'd expect from a team of flushers. There was one poor guy on the team, who shall remain nameless, who had been working on a platform across a sewer main that was blocked solid with doo-doo, and the platform gave way. Yes – he went straight into the murky depths below. Fortunately for him, he had the foresight to close his mouth and pinch his nose as he fell. Naturally, his comrades scrambled to rescue him. Having described in graphic detail the smell and feel of having your body completely covered in poo, he offered me a sandwich for lunch. Fantastic timing! This was typical of these boys, though. All of them had at least ten years' sewer experience, and accepted that the job needed doing, lunch needed eating, and that was that.

It was fascinating to hear from them exactly how they had ended up doing the job, and how their partners had become immune to the stench coming into the house at the end of every day. One chap had seen an advert in a local job centre for a labourer. Now, in my book, labourer is stretching the truth just a bit too far, don't you think? Anyway, he went for the interview and was told by a very prim operative from Thames Water personnel that 'The job will require you to be able to work all hours, in the open, and there's a lot of street digging involved. Can you handle this?' Needless to say, he was more than happy to accept the challenge, providing the pay cheques kept coming. What the middle- aged lady hadn't explained to the unsuspecting recruit was that he would be working on the road team for no more than about three weeks before being sent down the drains. Ten years later he's still going down there. Madness. I think I might have gone looking for the personnel operative and invited her to join me on a guided tour of my working environment – without the assistance of tiger balm.

I was also told that they used to assist the Metropolitan Police Anti-Terrorist Squad, in searching and sealing the drains in preparation for State occasions such as the State Opening of Parliament. That was an aspect of the job I hadn't considered. Nowadays, they simply provide safety cover to the police, who carry out the work on their own. They also assist the London Fire Brigade with rescues when necessary, although I still haven't worked out what a member of the public might be doing in the drains to need rescuing from them in the first place.

By now a terrific thunderstorm had engulfed the lorry, and it was difficult to see through the steamed-up windows. But too soon the call came, 'Embankment, all change, please.' As I crept out of the lorry on to a now sunny street, the whole team had big grins on their faces. 'What – what is it?' I asked, not really wanting to know.

'Over 'ere, lad, this is it, down 'ere.' Kenny was gesturing towards another hole in the ground.

'Boy, what a stink! Oh, that's too much. No, forget it, I'm not going down there for anybody.' The odour that filled the air this time was like nothing on earth. I wish I had one of those scratch-and-sniff cards for you to get an idea of the truly breathtaking stench. Pedestrians were giving both it and us a very wide berth. How unusual!

How can I describe the smell to you? Well, that's a tricky one. Imagine standing on a pig farm just as they are clearing up the slurry, add the smell of a large vat of cooking oil going off, a pinch of stagnant rainwater with, of course, rotting vegetation, and you might just be getting a feel for how awful it really was. 'C'mon, boy, you've done so well up till now, and this is as bad as it gets. You can't shy away,' implored Kenny.

At this point, I should have been walking briskly in the opposite direction towards the nearest tube station, like a participant in the London Marathon, but, oh, no, not me! Like a proper Charlie, I replied, 'You're absolutely right, I'm not going to let this job get the better of me. I'm supposed to be assessing you all for the title of Toughest Job, so I really should just get on with it.'

'Exactly,' came the unanimous response.

I slapped on another large dose of tiger balm, and ventured down the very short ladder to be met by walls caked in solidified fat crawling with cockroaches. By now the stench was beyond belief. Where on earth – no, correction – where in *hell* had I ended up? This, Kenny reliably informed me, was 'one of the main fat traps' and went on to explain that it was the one job that none of them liked. Believe me, I could see why. Two of the lads placed the noxious-gas detectors in strategic positions, then one passed me a shovel and said, 'Right, this is where the fun starts.'

I should explain to you all that I was standing in a fairly large hole approximately thirty feet long and fifteen wide. It was arranged on two levels, and was designed to catch all the fat that people pour down their drains – shame on you all, especially the restaurateurs out there who are guilty of the heinous crime! I was on the first level of the trap next to the mechanism that opened and shut the trap gate. Below, closer to Hades than you can imagine, Kenny was in the tank where the fat collected. The sight of everything imaginable petrified in large blocks of fat was gross – in fact, more horrific even than the smell.

'So, Kenny, what needs to be done here, mate, dare I ask?'

There was a long pause before Kenny replied, 'D'you know? Your luck ain't 'arf in today, Jeremy! All the storm water that's gushed down 'ere means that if we start shovelling this to ease the flow again, the gases are going to rocket through the roof, so we won't be able to do any real work.'

Thank you, God! I knew someone had been watching over me to make sure I didn't end up having to do anything too disgusting. The reality was that if we had started to disturb the vast wedge of fat and excrement, we would have been overcome by the noxious gases that live in such places, and might have needed rescuing. But while I'd been let off the hook, these boys would have to return at some point to this little delight with shovels and pickaxes to chip and shift the horrendous lump of awfulness, which might take them weeks! It was clear to me that they did an amazing job under horrible circumstances, and that I didn't really need to get dirty proving it to myself or, for that matter, the viewers watching the show.

Relief doesn't begin to describe how I felt to be back at street level. Then Kenny told me of a mile-long tunnel just four feet high that had become completely blocked by fat. It took the entire team of thirty-nine men, working in turn round the clock, a staggering nine months to clear it. Can you imagine chipping away with hand tools at that mess, just to get the water flowing again? The tunnels are so narrow that you have to rely entirely on sheer brute force and a shovel. Sadly, there's no high-tech solution to this problem, although experiments have been performed with various bacteria to see if the micro-organisms can eat away the blockage. However, everything thus far has failed to shift it. But, of course, the boys' daily battle against the gunk might be avoided if people simply refrained from pouring fat down the plug-hole in the first place!

We headed back to the depot via another drain. This time, we found ourselves in a four-foot-high tunnel, used to carry away rainwater from the street above. Do you remember me mentioning the Victorian Metropolitan Board of Works who had responsibility for the development of sewers? Well, it was they who decided that four-foot-high tunnels were just the right size for a man to work in. Clearly these fools had never met me, had they?

The drain was filling up rapidly, on account of the earlier torrential downpour overhead, as I followed Kenny down the ladder and started to make my way along the quarter-mile stretch to the next exit. 'Kenn—' was all I could say, as I lost my footing and ended up submerged in water – which, thankfully, was free of anything too unpleasant. But Denis had been right on my tail, and managed this time to capture my embarrassment for posterity.

Suffice it to say, this was the icing on the cake, and after nine hours on the go, admittedly without any strenuous work, the sewers had beaten me. I was ready to go home! 'That's it, Gary, I've had a gutful of this. I'm going back to the depot, and I don't want to see another drain for some considerable time to come.' Poor Gary couldn't get a word in edgeways as I trotted off down the street with one of my new flushing comrades.

Standing in the showers back at the depot, trying to scrub the stench out of my skin and hair, I had nothing but respect for the great team of guys I had had the pleasure to work with. There can be no doubt in my mind that sewer-flushers throughout the country are dedicated people, whom the rest of us take for granted. How often have you strolled past a gutter and really given any thought to what might be going on beneath your feet?

We're very lucky to have such an efficient system of waste disposal, but it's not so sophisticated that we can dispense with sending men down to keep the waters flow-ing. Without these unsung heroes we might well see scenes like those of sixteenth-century Britain where excrement passed along at street level. The boys of the nation's sewers deserve the public's recognition and gratitude. It is truly unpleasant below our pavements and I, for one, would not want to swap places with any of the flushers I met. This is definitely very close to the top of the list of jobs that really are Britain's Toughest!

# chapter two
# FISH MERCHANT

**Salary:** £9,000–23,000, depending on age and experience

**Requirements:** Applicants need to be physically fit, capable of working unsociable hours and not object to strong odours. In addition, they should possess a thick skin, and not be easily offended by the BOSS!

**Toughness rating:** 10

Arriving at work for a two a.m. shift is most people's idea of a living nightmare, and quite rightly too! Actually, I'm used to early starts, but even I was beginning to wonder what persuaded anyone to come to work at this ungodly hour, as I hunted around Billingsgate's car park for Maggie Barton.

Maggie, I was told by my researcher Leceia Gordon, is married to one of Billingsgate's sixty-five traders. In fact, her husband Roger has been a fixture at the London market for more than twenty-five years. According to Leceia, whom

I've always thought to be such a lovely girl, 'Roger can be a bit difficult to work for, and you should be prepared for what may turn out to be the hardest two days' work ever.' There was no need for me to reply, as my less than enthusiastic frown told Leceia all she needed to know about how over-joyed I was at the prospect of two days' hard graft. Give me a break here, folks, it was just after two o'clock in the morning!

'Jeremy, hi, I'm Maggie.' The authoritative voice came from a slight woman clutching a brand new white hat and an overall, which she thrust into my hand. 'Put 'em on, got to get started.'

Oh, boy, this was my cue to get working. Now, it should be explained at this point that it's customary when meeting the main contributor, or character, of any film to spend a little time chatting about how the filming will work, what sort of things need to be covered, not to be nervous, etc., etc. But for some reason Maggie didn't have time for idle chit-chat, let alone worrying about the camera. 'Come on, there's work to be done before the boss arrives and there's no time for chat-ter!' she said – I'd been hoping, as always, that I'd have a short break for coffee before starting work.

As we entered the building, which had been a warehouse up until 1982 when it was renovated into today's market, it was immediately obvious to me that I was entering a very fishy plaice – oops, sorry, couldn't resist it. The smell reminded me of those cockle-and-mussel stalls in seaside towns up and down the country, but intensified by several thousand per cent. It was certainly a shock to the nostrils.

As I looked around the market, which had traded on London's Lower Thames Street for more than nine hundred years before it moved to its present location adjacent to Canary Wharf in the Docklands area, it struck me that very few people were about. It had been explained to me that Maggie and the team were nearly always the first traders to arrive at the market, because Roger was so demanding and had such exacting standards – the early bird catching the worm and all that stuff.

Had I not been so used to dealing with all sorts of truculent people, I might have started to develop a fear of the mysterious Roger. This man was sounding more and more fearsome! Maggie informed me that my day would be divided into three specific jobs, with the first task being preparation of Roger's stall. Where was Roger? I hear you ask. And it's a damn good question. Surely if Roger wanted his stall to be ready for trading, he should have been at Billingsgate supervising, don't you think? Apparently not. According to Maggie, Roger didn't get home until after midnight most nights of the week, and he needed at least three hours' sleep before travelling back along the A13 from their home near Southend-on-Sea, to the market.

'Maggie, sorry, but why on earth does Roger get home so late?' I asked while trying to lug boxes of cod towards the stall from the storage area outside.

'He does the dogs at Romford,' was Maggie's response before she encouraged me to work a bit harder: 'Come on, Jeremy, time's running out and Roger will soon be here.' There was no time to go into what 'the dogs' meant – Roger would soon be arriving and Maggie seemed somewhat disturbed that the stall was less than ready. Who did this Roger think he was, anyway?

By four the market was buzzing like a mainline railway station at the height of the rush hour, people milling around in different directions frantically trying to avoid getting caught in queues. Everything felt slightly surreal: the majority of London was still asleep, and we had already been hard at it for two hours. My beautiful white coat was covered in blood and guts, and stank to high heaven of, yes, you guessed it . . . what else but FISH!

A quick glance around the expanse of stalls revealed a scene of good honest East End men getting ready for a hard day's fish selling. Maggie appeared to be the only woman there, and I began to wonder what it must be like for her to work in this male-dominated club. It was obvious that she needed to flex her muscles to demonstrate to the men that she could do this job with her eyes shut. I for one was not going to challenge her for supremacy of the Barton fish-trading empire.

With just ten minutes to go before the boss was due to arrive, I managed to persuade Maggie to give up worrying about the state of the stall – after all, she could blame it on me if Roger was unhappy – and pop for a cuppa into the market's permanent café.

It was a bit like the Bridge Street Café in *EastEnders*, and when we went in I was immediately aware of the respect the other traders had for Maggie. There was the usual banter you might expect from market traders, but the men accepted her as one of them and had general chit-chats with her about the state of business.

'So, Maggs, how will the rest of the day shape up, then?' I enquired eagerly, wanting to hear when it might be over. 'We'll help Roger and the boys with the sales until about seven, and then we'll have to load up the van ready for the deliveries,' she replied.

Deliveries? Now, clearly my second task was to help Roger, a prospect with which I was not overjoyed, but the third sounded like Delivery Boy.

As we rushed back to the stall, Maggie gave me a rundown of her average working day: 'As you know, I'm up at just after midnight – in fact, not long after Roger gets into bed – to get on my way to Billingsgate. After setting up the stall I help Roger until seven, then pop round the market buying fish supplies that we don't have on our own stall, like crabs and eels, then load up my van and make deliveries to our restaurant customers. At about three p.m., I get back to the house to wash the van out, then feed and exercise my horse. After that it's back to the house to feed Roger.'

'Enough already, Maggie, I'm exhausted just thinking about it!' When we got back to the market, the whole place was buzzing with excitement and laughter. What was happening to cause such a stir? 'Look out, Roger's on the way,' shouted one of the fearsome fish trader's staff.

Although I should have been terrified at the sight of Roger, I couldn't help but laugh: Indiana Jones, no less, was standing before me. How many of you can remember Harrison Ford in *Raiders of the Lost Ark*? Harrison played this all-action hero who went everywhere in fatigues and that great big adventurer's hat. Well, no word of a lie, Roger was dressed in such a fashion, hat and all, and the only thing that appeared to be missing was Harrison's trusty whip, although it would soon become apparent that he didn't need a whip, oh, no – his tongue was more than capable of lashing people into action!

In almost stereotypical market-trader fashion, Roger spoke in a real gor-blimey voice – indeed 'Wotcha, boy,' was the nicest thing he said to me within the confines of Britain's biggest fish market. Maggie had warned me that Roger didn't like slackers and that few new recruits lasted more than one shift with Billingsgate's very own Indiana, and she hadn't been kidding: this man was unbelievable. People are normally on their best behaviour when camera crews are about, but if I witnessed Roger at his best, I'd hate to have seen him at his worst! 'There's more life on you than in you, bleedin' Nora, get a bloody move on. The fish might be dead, but you ain't.' Roger was trying to encourage me to go outside to the storage area to collect bags of clams for one of his best customers.

In all my years of dealing with staff, I'd never tried this interesting method of getting the work done. 'All right, all right, I'm going! Honestly, there's no need to be abusive,' was about all I could muster by way of a response.

Maggie sensed the inevitable showdown brewing between myself and Roger, and quickly ushered me towards the storage area. 'Is he always so pleasant to his staff?' I asked weakly. 'Oh, Jeremy, he's being nice to you at the moment,' she grinned.

What made a woman want to work in a place like this for a man like Roger – let alone be married to him, for heaven's sake? Maggie was not only in love with Roger but with her job too. She enthused all the time about the atmosphere that exists at Billingsgate. 'This place is electric. Although we're all competing against one another there's a real sense of family. Everyone has got something to say about Roger and his ways, not that you'd want to hear most of it. We work harder than most, which has made Roger successful – and that occasionally makes some a bit green with envy. Most of the people in here, however, are the salt of the earth, and if ever you had a crisis you could rely on them to give a helping hand.'

As I glanced around the trading hall, I could see that between the traders there was fierce but pleasant competition, but none of this seemed enough to convince me that Maggie really loved her lifestyle. She was adamant that Roger was actually a big softie and that just under the surface lay a warm, generous man. Sure, there seemed to be something between them, and although he shouted at her as much as he did at the rest of us, including the other traders, she never had a bad word to say about him.

However: 'F*** me, how long does it take to get a few f****** clams?' was what greeted us when we got back to the stall empty-handed. 'Where are the bleedin' clams?' bellowed my new boss.

Strangely enough, now seemed like the ideal opportunity to ask what attributes were needed to be a successful employee of the Barton stall. 'F*** me, boy, you want to talk about a load of old s*** when we've got fish to sell? There's more life in Nelson's column than you've got!' Obviously, this *wasn't* a good time to chat about things that would normally come up in an interview. 'Where are those bleedin' clams?' he roared.

Maggie grabbed me by the arm and pulled me away to start weighing salmon for one of the regular buyers, thus saving me from a further barracking from the boss.

A man who had pitched up at the stall was getting the usual friendly Roger Barton service: 'Don't maul the bleedin' fish, for Christ's sake, man. If you ain't gonna buy it, get your bleedin' mitts off it.'

Why buy fish from this man? I hear you ask. Good question, although the quality of the fish on the stall was, according to other traders, very good. The poor unsuspecting member of the public had wanted to buy some kind of tropical fish I'd never heard of. 'Mind them bleedin' fins for f*** sake, Jeremy, they're as sharp as hell,' was Roger's friendly advice as I attempted to sell the man his fish.

Fish gills are just one of the many hazards that surround those working in the market, as I discovered when I was walking back from the storage area. John, the film director, had asked me for my thoughts on the job so far. As I started to talk I walked straight into one of the barrows used to haul the fish around the market, and went flying through the air to land rather ungracefully on my bum, putting an enormous dent in my pride, much to the amusement of the surrounding traders. Fortunately, this was one of those moments of considerable embarrassment that was edited out of the final programme.

It would be fair to say that after just two hours of being with Roger I was more than ready to escape the market to help Maggie with her restaurant deliveries. Before we left, Maggie showed me round the market and introduced me to some of the characters that made a living there. 'How you gettin' on with that bleedin' Roger, then, Jeremy? Gor, he's a one, ain't he? Still, he flogs the fish, dun' he!' These were the jocular comments of one shellfish trader.

'Blimey, mate, you've got yer work cut out for yer on that old Barton stall! How's it goin'?' asked another fun-loving purveyor of fish.

Most, if not all, seemed really pleasant people who just liked having a laugh, admittedly on this occasion at me for ending up working with Roger, who they all felt at times was a bit over the top. I felt as though I was caught in the middle of the musical adaptation of Charles Dickens's *Oliver Twist*. Can you remember the scene when Oliver first arrives in London and is shown round the market by the Artful Dodger? Well, maybe Billingsgate was the source of Dickens's inspiration when he wrote about the friendly atmosphere that exists in such places.

Our last port of call was a specialist trader who sold nothing but eels. Ugh, I hate snakes, and these slimy little blighters are very similar. I was amazed to learn, however, that in 1699 Parliament passed an Act making Billingsgate 'a free and open market selling all sorts of fish whatsoever', with the exception of eels, which could only be sold by Dutch fishermen who moored their boats on the Thames. Does this seem daft? Well, the Dutch had helped feed the people of London after the Great Fire, and this Act guaranteed them an income. Needless to say, this has long since changed, and the trader bagging up Maggie's half-dozen eels was most certainly an East End lad.

There is sanctuary in Maggie's life, but not at home where you might expect it. No, it comes in the shape of her maroon VW van. Once inside her little refrigerated transporter, she is free from the macho world of Billingsgate, where she works harder than most of the men put together. Escaping the fish, however, is more difficult. We'd packed the van full of marine delights, which had to be delivered to her restaurant customers by twelve noon in order for them to be able to offer the catch of the day, so to speak, on their lunch-time menus.

The pressure is on for Maggie to deliver to ten or so restaurants in the southern part of Essex, who all want their fish as soon as she leaves Billingsgate between seven-thirty and eight a.m. Now, anyone who has tried driving along the A13 towards Southend, or for that matter the A127, at any time of day, will know how slow the route can be. You only need one breakdown to set the cat among the pigeons and you're in a jam for hours. So, it's vital for Maggie to work her way through the hold-ups in a calm and efficient manner, which, as you might expect of a woman married to Roger, she does without difficulty. She really is a one-woman army, capable of coping with anything that gets thrown at her.

As we went from restaurant to restaurant, I could see why Maggie was so attentive to this aspect of her job. The clients really appreciated her knowledge of fish. 'The sea bass is good today,' she told one Italian chef, who was busy pressing the espresso coffee-maker into action to wet our parched throats. Although we didn't get to all the restaurants before noon, the customers were relaxed and all offered us refreshment, which certainly beat life in Docklands being abused by Indiana. Except for one: he was clearly struggling with the English language and accused me of giving him sea bass when he wanted skate. I gave up trying to decipher his dulcet tones, and Maggie stepped in – only to be equally frustrated by his less than coherent manner.

The confusion had been caused by Leceia who, as we'd entered the restaurant, had been chatting to me about sea bass, and how she fancied some for dinner. The little chef – no, really, he was very short and looked a little bit like the emblem used on those roadside cafés – thought we were discussing the sea bass we had put into his order.

Finally at three o'clock, having gone via the stables where Maggie keeps her horse, we reached the hub of the Barton fish empire – home. A pair of gloves and a brush were thrust into my weary hands. 'There you go. If you can scrub and disinfect the back of the van I'll go and start dinner for us all.' What was really annoying was that Maggie seemed so lively, while I was ready to drop. Her husband was fast asleep in bed.

Asleep! Who did he think he was, sleeping at a time like this, while I was left with *two* blessed fish-infested vans – one was Roger's – to scrub, and his poor wife was chained to the kitchen sink peeling potatoes? What was going on here?

Can you believe it? Roger starts work at Billingsgate between three to four a.m. each working day, leaves the market at one, heads home for a bit of sleep, and then is off to Romford to be a bookie at the dog track in the evening. He must be mad! I hear you say. Yes, quite probably. But Maggie leads an equally exhausting life, never resting for more than four hours a day. While Roger is at the dogs, she's often on the phone for hours at night, trying to buy fish supplies for the next day's trading. This can be trickier that it sounds when little fish is being caught by our hard-pressed fishermen.

Were they worried about money? 'No, not really, we're very lucky our business has been successful, but this is because Roger expects us all to work hard and to almost perfect standards,' Maggie explained, as she prepared the fish for dinner. Yes, I've been surrounded by fish all day, and Roger has decided he would like me to sample his wares for dinner. Cheers, Roger!

'Jeremy, would you mind popping upstairs to wake Roger? There's a cup of tea and his paper, he'll want that. Oh, and by the way, don't shout, he hates it as he wakes up.' Too late, I was already steaming up the rather steep staircase towards the tomb where my Genghis Khan-like boss was resting, determined to wake him in a manner befitting a fog-horn on a large ocean-going liner. '*Wake up, Roger!*', I yelled, having no fear of the consequences.

'Oh, is it time to get up?' asked Roger, in a polite, demure manner.

Sorry, what's this? Roger being nice to me? Surely not!

Sitting in the dining room, listening to Roger telling us about his life, it became clear why Maggie liked him. This was not the Roger of Billingsgate: he was pleasant, caring and, above all, attentive to his more-than-overworked wife. Wearing his striped dressing-gown, not wanting to spill anything on his bookies' togs, he regaled us with stories of his twenty-five years in the fish trade, and how you needed to be hard-faced for people not to 'try and put one over you'. There was probably a lot of truth in those few words, and his brash unwelcoming manner had probably ensured his success. Personally, I didn't much like his management tech-niques, although in his home, surrounded by the things he liked, I had nothing but respect for him.

'Jeremy, you've shocked me, ain't you? You've worked really hard, and if ever you fancy a longer spell on the stall, let me know.' This, from Roger, was a real compliment, but I was still trying to figure out what drove Maggie to work such horrendous hours, knowing that she only had Sunday on which to sit back and relax. I guess I can only conclude that she is a real Trojan. Wonder Woman springs to mind. Maggie's social life is almost non-existent and her nocturnal activities are alien to the majority of us. Few would swap places with her.

# chapter three
# TURKEY INSEMINATOR

**Salary:** £15,000–23,000 per annum or thereabouts

**Requirements:** Applicants should enjoy working outside, not be afraid of animals, enjoy hard work, but above all have plenty of puff.

**Toughness rating: 9**

As with most of the films in this series, it all started with a phone call from the production office. 'Go to Danbury,' I was told. 'It's only a short hop from home, so you'll be able to have a few extra hours' sleep for a change.' So far so good! 'You're heading for Kelly's Farm,' Zoë, the production secretary, continued.

'Oh? What's there?' I asked.

'Just a few free-range turkeys,' she answered jovially.

Did she know something I didn't? For sure! But she wasn't about to let on.

'What's in store for me this time, Zoë?'

'Hmmmmm . . . all will be revealed.' By now she was

having a right old laugh at my expense. What on earth could be so funny? Surely feeding a bunch of free-range turkeys couldn't be difficult, could it? Presumably you just throw a bit of grain on the ground, then watch them cluck round happy as Larry?

Before I had time to think about what might happen during the day, I was pulling up alongside a group of large sheds at the farm. As I opened the car door, the dawn chorus of tuneless turkeys greeted me. The noise was, quite frankly, deafening! The din reminded me a bit of the occasions when I used to have to announce a delay at Heathrow Airport, when the assembled hordes of passengers would all rant and rave in a similarly high-pitched tone, bless them. For some reason, though, I felt that crowd control of turkeys was going to prove a great deal more difficult than it was with a few irate passengers.

My crew, Denis, Paul, Stuart and Gary, the same poor bunch who had had the pleasure of going into London's sewers with me, were standing by one of the sheds, and informed me, 'You're looking for Paul Kelly, mate!' Never mind that they had dispensed with the usual polite British greeting of 'Good morning', they all wore grins the size of the Severn Bridge. Without doubt these boys knew what was about to happen and, in true *Toughest Job* style, were not about to let the poor old presenter, yours truly, in on the gag! No surprises there, then!

I opened the shed door, which had restriction warnings written all over it, and was greeted by a chap who seemed curiously overjoyed to see me. 'Hi, Jeremy, I'm Paul Kelly.'

Right, that was handy: at least I wasn't going to have to traipse around the farm looking for him – the film crew had instructed him to wait like a coiled spring for me behind the door.

When I say he looked overjoyed to see me, what I meant to say was that he appeared to have the devil in his eye, and

– not for the first time in the series, I can assure you – I began to feel like I'd been set right up for a fall. Especially when Paul handed me a pair of blue overalls and white wellies. What was about to happen, I had no idea.

Having dipped my wellies into a chemical bath, and scrubbed my hands in an alcohol solution, I was taken by Paul into the shed. Suddenly he started making strange gobbling noises at the four hundred or so turkeys I could see walking around before me. 'Gobble, gobble, gobble, gobble gobble!' Before I had a chance to enquire of him exactly what he was doing, the turkeys went mad! They were running round gobbling back at him with great ferocity. In fact, I can safely say I've never seen anything like it in my life. Sure, I'd witnessed countless late passengers running for flights in my former life working for Aeroflot, but this was unique.

'What's the story here, Paul? Why are these turkeys behaving like it's the first day of the Harrods January sale?' I asked.

'There are just over four hundred stag turkeys in here, and we are about to extract their sperm to inseminate the three thousand-plus hens we have on the other side of the pen!'

Oh, my word! Was the deafening sound of clucking birds making me hear things? 'Did you say "inseminate", Paul?' I asked with a quiver in my voice.

'Yep, that's right!' He was almost laughing with anticipation.

Now, for those of you who are interested and, yes, there must be a few, every turkey strutting its stuff around the globe can trace its ancestry back to just one wild breed of these rather strange-looking birds, who roamed northern Mexico and the eastern seaboard of the United States. It was sometime during the sixteenth century that they were introduced to Europe from over the Pond, although it wasn't until Victorian times that they became the nation's favourite on Christmas Day – the goose occupied pole position before then. If you aren't interested in such things, then I make no apology for wasting a bit of the book telling you about it – after all, you may be in a pub one day and a useless piece of information like this could win you a pint of beer in a quiz!

Right, back to business. 'Sorry . . . I still cannot get to grips with this, Paul. Surely you can let Mother Nature do her stuff? Can't we just go and feed a few in the field while the stags put a smile on the faces of the hens on their own?'

'No,' was his answer. What I hadn't considered at this point was that turkeys are polygamous, so the stags will fight among themselves for supremacy and access to the hens. Clearly, if you are running a business you can't afford to let your stags kill each other for the chance to meet three thousand-plus hens, can you? Let's face it, we wouldn't allow it to happen among humans, would we?

This thought was of no comfort to me as Paul dragged me further into the shed to meet one of his AI (artificial insemination) teams, led by Dave. 'Hi, Dave, you must be mad, mate!' I said.

The team all laughed as Paul, who had some rubber tubing in his hand, told them, 'Jeremy and I will join you in the hen shed later, but first I want to teach Jeremy how to extract the seed.'

No, no, no, no! Give me the stench of the London sewers any day. I simply couldn't bring myself to do this, no matter how important it was to show the British public just how tough being an inseminator was! This, Auntie BBC, was simply too much, one job too many, one laugh at my expense beyond the pale!

'Right, then, Jeremy,' uttered Paul, who by now was crouching on the floor surrounded by the source of his income, as I headed towards the exit. 'Come back here! It's as easy as one, two, three!' he called, as Gary, the director, made sure I couldn't leave the shed.

Great! I wasn't going to be able to avoid the inevitable insemination, which by its dictionary definition means to 'introduce semen into a female by natural or artificial means' – another less-than-helpful thought that filled my mind with fear. 'One, two, three you say, Paul? What if I have no desire to find out just how easy one, two, three is?'

Paul didn't bother to respond as he thrust at me a long thin piece of rubber hose with a test-tube attached to it. 'Put that here and suck,' he demanded. He was holding a stag and massaging its hindquarters.

'SUCK? Did you say SUCK? Don't be ridiculous! I'm not sucking this tube or anything else in here, thank you very much!' was my somewhat stressed response. My agony was bringing tears to the eyes of Denis and Paul, who were desperately trying to film without letting the camera wobble. 'Listen, *surely* it's better to let these fellas court the ladies on their own, isn't it? They don't need us to help them.'

'That may be true,' said Paul, 'but the success rate when the turkeys are left to their own devices is only around 62 per cent, while artificial insemination means a success rate in excess of 95 per cent. Not only this and the fact that the stags fight each other for the hens, but if you allow the stags to mate naturally with the hens, they have a tendency to scratch at the hen's hindquarters, which damages the flesh, making the hens unsuitable for sale.' This still wasn't enough to convince me to put the tube to my mouth. Do you blame me?

But it was no good, I was going to have to bite the bullet – or in this case the tube – and start sucking if I was going to be allowed to get home that night. 'Ugh – ugh – ugh – this is disgusting,' I said, with the thin rubber tube between my teeth, staring boss-eyed at the fluid moving rather rapidly towards the test-tube. Forgive me, but there was only one thing on my mind at this point: 'Have you ever swallowed any of this, Paul?' Well, I had to ask, didn't I? Wouldn't you, if you'd been put in the same situation?

'Several times, but it's nothing to worry about,' Paul responded, emphatically.

By now I'd dropped the tube and was having a discussion with Gary about the rationale behind dragging me to this quiet corner of Britain in search of a Tough Job. 'Do we really need to continue with this one? Have I not sucked enough?' begged yours truly.

'Sadly not, Jeremy. You know we need to cover all of the shots for the film,' explained Gary, who has this uncanny knack of making an order sound like a polite request.

When we're filming we have to get close-up shots, shots of me with the contributors – in this case Paul Kelly – shots from a distance, wide shots and generic shots, known as GVs – general views, which all come together to make a film. In fact a ten-minute film in this series, which is the average, can take up to three days to shoot, so you can imagine there was no way Gary was going to let me off with only one suck at the tube.

I sucked for a further hour and a half, much to the amusement of my crew. I'd sucked for Britain and then some more, and suddenly my heart pounded like a steam train, thundering along at full speed. 'Would you like to have a go at extracting here at the business end, Jeremy?' asked Paul, who was pushing against the boundaries of acceptability in my book.

'Sorry, but ever since I arrived here this morning I've been having terrible trouble with my ears! Are you suggesting I swap roles, and you suck the tube while I do the necessary down there?' I really didn't want him to answer but feared he would.

'There's nothing wrong with your hearing, Jeremy. If you want to be a successful turkey farmer you need to learn all the skills!' was Paul's astonishing reply – which, fortunately for me, Gary hadn't heard.

Now, I should explain that Paul, his sister Lynne and their parents Derek and Mollie have been successfully farming turkeys in Essex for more than thirty years. In 1983 they reintroduced the bronze breed of turkey back to the UK market from the US. If you know anything about turkeys you will appreciate that the bronze breed, according to some, is one of the fleshiest turkeys you can get, with incredibly moist meat. But this meant nothing to me as I looked down at the stags still busily gobbling at their master. 'Thanks, Paul, but I've never really considered a career as a turkey farmer. You won't mind if I turn your offer down? And, anyway, what makes you want to do this for a living?' I was trying to distract him so that Gary didn't cotton on to the suggestion that I swap places with him. To be honest, though, Paul didn't need to reply: the farmhouse he shared with his wife and children told even the slowest of onlookers that there was money to be made from turkey farming.

However, he said, 'Financially it can be very rewarding, providing you maintain the quality that customers expect, which is why we inseminate. Right then, Jeremy, your turn!' Damn, my ploy hadn't worked. In fact, in the end I had to refuse to swap places with Paul, which, thankfully, Gary, being the true professional that he is, accepted. Phew, a narrow escape . . . I'm sorry, but there are some things you shouldn't have to do to prove a job is *tough*.

Having survived the trauma of the extraction, I headed with Paul into an adjacent shed to catch up with Dave and his team. What greeted me? Only about twelve hundred of Paul's turkeys. They were gurgling and gobbling in all the wrong places as far as I was concerned. They appeared happy, though, and they spent their lives wandering around in open fields and sheds, rather than being trapped in coops.

Above the din of the hens I asked of Dave, 'Sorry, but what gets you out of bed in the mornings to come here? I can understand why Paul does this, but you and the boys – I've no idea!'

'Generally it's the wife who gets me out of bed, mate!' came Dave's witty reply.

All right, I did ask for it. 'No, I mean why do you do this job?' I continued, ignoring the laughter of his colleagues.

'We only do this artificial insemination job for fourteen weeks of the year,' he said. It transpired that each hen was artificially inseminated by Dave and the team once a week during that period. After this, each hen will lay an average of four eggs. Even for people like me who can't add up to save their lives, that's a lot of turkeys, especially when you multiply the figure by the more than three thousand hens on the farm.

'What do you lads do for the rest of the year, then?' I asked.

Dave, who seemed to be doing all the talking simply because the others were laughing so much at the faces I was pulling, answered, 'We're busy most of the time assisting Paul to fatten up the turkeys ready for killing, plucking and packing for our busiest time of the year.'

Yes! You guessed it! Christmas!

Still bemused I asked, 'I still don't really understand why you do this job. On a scale of one to ten for weird and yucky careers, this probably rates an eight?'

'I've been here a while now, and really enjoy it. It's near to home, and the money's pretty good. We have a right old laugh here most days – you just have to remember not to suck too hard.' The boys laughed like drains.

I'd been chatting so much with the boys that I hadn't realized what time it was until Paul said, 'Right, Jeremy, we'll have to sort the hens out this afternoon, I'm afraid, and you've been talking so much we're behind schedule. But I'd like you to come to the house for lunch.' As we left the shed, he instructed Dave and his team to store the morning's semen collections in preparation for the afternoon session with the hens.

'What's on the menu for lunch?' This has to be one of the most stupid questions I have ever asked.

'Poultry!' came Paul's predictable reply. 'Not turkey, though, Jeremy, I'm not that cruel. I'd like you to try a new line in chicken we're introducing.' It was very kind of Paul to offer me lunch, but the morning's activities had almost convinced me to become a vegetarian. Still, time in the house was going to give me the chance to chat with Debbie, his elegant wife, who works for a fashion designer in London.

'Debbie, when you first met Paul, did he tell you what he did for a living?' was my first question.

'The first time we met was in a bar in town and I can't say that he did tell me about his occupation. If I remember rightly, he just skipped over the subject.' Then Debbie explained, 'It took him a few weeks to own up, and when I heard what he did, my immediate reaction was one of curiosity rather than disgust.'

That was fair enough, I thought. 'So, Debbie, have you ever helped Paul in the sheds at this time of year?'

'No! You won't catch me out there. I'm quite happy commuting to London to work. I wouldn't be any good at farming anyway,' Debbie replied. I can't say I disagreed with her - in fact, she seemed the most sane person I'd met all day.

Paul had been listening to his wife's interview, but stated adamantly, 'I love the job. It's very rewarding when a customer comes back every year to buy their Christmas turkey from you.'

There we had it: Paul loved his job, and who was I to argue with him? I'll confess at this point that interviewing the couple within the confines of their kitchen had made me hungry. Come on, cut me some slack here, folks, please! The kitchen had filled with the aroma of freshly roasted chicken. 'I know I shouldn't, Paul, especially not after this morning, but I'll try a bit, if you don't mind.'

No sooner had I finished giving my critique on the chicken, which tasted as good as it smelt, than Paul was ushering me back towards the sheds. Dave and the team greeted us clutching dozens of test tubes, all containing the fruits of our labours from earlier in the day – or should I say the fruits of the stags' labours? Anyway, my nightmare continued as Paul demonstrated exactly how to inseminate the hens. 'This is another of those simple tasks, Jeremy.'

'Don't tell me, like one, two, three!'

Paul nodded as he blew like fury down a new piece of tubing. Once he'd dispatched the all-important seed, he continued, 'Watch as the hen walks off. If you do the job right she'll shake her tail violently as she goes. That's the sign that you've hit the spot!'

'Oh, behave yourself! Enough, please. I really don't want to know any more – that's far too much information already, Paul, thank you very much,' I exclaimed.

I was permitted to watch Paul and Dave for a further five minutes, as I protested, 'I want to get it right – after all, I don't want to disappoint the hens, now do I?'

The entire film crew were laughing their heads off at me. Then, 'No more stalling, Jeremy. Come on, mate, the sooner you do this the sooner we can all go home,' came the sobering but correct words of Denis, my great cameraman buddy.

Paul decided that the quickest way to get the job over and done with would be for him to stimulate the hens, something I'm not going to describe here for the sake of decency. I would then deposit the seed in the correct place, under Paul's supervision. Having reached this compromise, I agreed, somewhat foolhardily, to give it a whirl. 'Right, here goes, the first hen, please.' I was trying to sound like I could cope with this. After all, this task is performed all over the world by farmers – in fact, somewhere around 20 million turkeys are bred in the US alone each year using similar methods. Staggering, wouldn't you agree?

'Remember to blow and not suck this time, Jeremy,' was Paul's little pearl of wisdom as I prepared to start the process of fertilizing the hen that was being held in front of me.

'Blow! You're not kidding! I'm going to blow! Never fear, that much I can remember!' came my emphatic reply, as I blew with great gusto down the tube.

'Success!' declared Paul, as Denis swooped round with the camera just in time to catch the hen shaking her tail, indicating her delight at my technique. I blew for a further hour while we gathered the shots, during which time I had 'made a lot of hens happy', in Paul's words.

By three o'clock I'd had enough, and was mighty glad to hear Gary shout, 'That's a *wrap*,' which signalled the end of my trauma. I could go home.

As I drove away from the farm, I was left wondering what was so tough about it all. Sure, I'd managed to suck and blow in all the right places, and if you don't particularly like the thought of the job it might be difficult. And, yes, you needed to be a particular type of person to want to earn a living – which I hasten to add was pretty good – in such a manner. But tough? No, not really! Unpleasant? For sure!

# chapter four
# KNIFE-THROWING CIRCUS PERFORMER

**Salary:** £70–120 per week

**Requirements:** Applicants should have a flexible, versatile approach to their work, be adaptable to any situation and happy to perform in public. Above all, they should lack any sense of fear.

**Toughness rating: 9**

Like many kids, I used to enjoy visiting the circus, although I have to confess I never really fancied running away with one, much preferring the creature comforts of home and my mum's cooking. However, I was challenged to join a circus act called Los Alexandros, and spend two days learning the skills of a performer and absorbing myself in the lifestyle of a professional travelling showman. Was I going to enjoy it, and did I think it would be tough? If I'm honest, I didn't have a clue what to expect.

I arrived at a deserted racecourse not far from Taunton in Somerset at eight o'clock one morning to find the Big Top of Jay Miller's Circus in front of me. Nicky, the film's director, had described it to me as a small, friendly, family-run business. I was looking for Tex Alexandros and his partner Julie Bradford, who had worked together for Jay Miller's for more than twelve years.

The Big Top was encircled by the mobile homes of the showmen, reminding me of the wild west film about Custer's Last Stand where wagons had been set to protect our hero and his men from the Indians. Was this about to be my last stand? I, in true *Toughest Job* style, had a feeling it might be.

As I stumbled around the ground knocking on every caravan door and waking people up in my search for Tex and Julie, I was greeted by Russians (fantastic – gave me a chance to chinwag in Russian), Hungarians, Ukrainians, Moldovans and, of course, one or two Brits. I ought to explain that the circus has had a long tradition in Eastern Europe, and that since the collapse of the Soviet Union a large number of highly trained performers have found themselves working seasonal contracts in Britain. So, it wasn't a huge surprise for me to find the odd comrade knocking around, especially as they are now able to travel freely (subject to visa regulations), and earn money wherever they can. During the Communist era they had only been able to travel overseas as part of an entire circus, and then only if the State security apparatus could guarantee every individual's return home. Although the circus is still an important part of the culture in countries like Russia, financial pressures force many performers to work overseas.

After several cups of Bodrost Chai, a brand of Russian tea, I was shown where to find Tex and Julie by Oleg –

pronounced Arleg – a high-wire gymnast from Moldova who was built like the proverbial brick outhouse, if you catch my drift. *'No spasibo, Oleg, skoro uvidimsya'* – Thanks, Oleg, see you later. I knocked gingerly on the door of Tex and Julie's home. Why gingerly? Simple – I'd been warned that Tex was handy with knives.

'Come on in, Jeremy.' It was Tex, a slight man with his hair in a ponytail, who greeted me. 'I'd like you to meet Julie, and over here is Leone, our daughter.' Julie, who was then four months pregnant with their second child, was frantically trying to get Leone ready for school. 'Does she have lessons here with the other circus children?' I asked.

'No, no, all the children attend whichever local school is nearest to the venues where we are performing,' I was told. Apparently, there is an organization that assists travelling performers to arrange schooling for their children – it sounds like an absolute godsend.

'Julie, isn't it difficult for Leone to make friends, though, if she's moving from place to place?' I asked. 'Come to think of it, how do you yourselves keep in touch with your mates?'

Julie responded without hesitation: 'If you take a look out of the window, you'll see that a number of families travel with this circus, and most of the children are a similar age to Leone, which is great as they all play together. As for us, well, that's not so easy. We're on the move for three-quarters of the year, and it's rare for either Tex or me to get home to see our relatives, although we do manage the odd letter. The mobile phone has been a real revelation for us. The good thing about our situation, though, is that everyone here in the circus helps each other. It's one big family, so you never feel as though friends are lacking.'

Making the most of the opportunity to chat, I asked, 'Do you ever get bored of living in the caravan? Don't you sometimes crave a nice semi somewhere?'

'Yeah, sure, who wouldn't? It can sometimes be a bit claustrophobic in here, but then again we don't have the pressure of a mortgage – this thing's paid for!' Although everything they said made sense, I was already getting a feeling for just how tough it is to maintain a normal family routine when you are constantly on the move.

'Dare I ask what's first for me, then?' I enquired, with a glance at Tex's filthy hands.

'Well,' he said, with a grin, 'there's loads of maintenance stuff that needs to be looked at. Once we've cleared a few of those jobs, we can start to teach you some of the skills you'll need for tomorrow's two shows.'

Wait a second! No one had said anything about me appearing in any show, let alone performing! But there was no time for me to make further enquiries because I was dragged off with my camera crew towards a host of show vehicles at the entrance to the Big Top.

As we started to feed cables from a generator towards the tent – oops, I've been told off for calling it a tent: I mean the Big Top, of course – Tex started to educate me in the history of the circus. Believe it or not, the modern circus as we know it can be traced back to a chap called Philip Astley, a cavalryman who left the British Army in 1768 to perform as a trickrider in London. So successful was his show that in 1772 he began to tour Europe with other acts. He is reputed to have established the first circus in Russia, performing in 1793 at the Winter Palace in St Petersburg. But one thing's for sure: Mr Astley certainly started the trend for a traditional feature of horsemanship in circus performances across the globe, and in fact the word 'circus' derives from the circular arena used by these horsemen.

Tex, who hails from the West Midlands, explained, 'My dad led a troupe of horsemen called the the Congress of Roughriders, who toured with the Buffalo Bill Wild West

Show. I learnt horsemanship from my dad, and still love the Cossack-style trick riding, which as you probably know is all about being able to ride facing backwards, under the horse, hanging from its tail and jumping on and off while it's on the move.' Tex looked sad when he spoke of his dad, whom he had clearly respected and admired, but before I had a chance to ask him any more, he said, 'Come on, Jeremy, we need to get the men organized to change the tyres on these lorries before I show you a bit of rope-spinning.'

I should explain that Tex not only headed up the Los Alexandros act but also supervised all the ongoing maintenance and repair jobs for the circus. Which, when you consider it involved mobilizing the Moldovan assistants, whose command of English was restricted to the pidgin version, was not a simple task. Luckily for me, they had an excellent command of Russian, and for the first time I felt of some use as I asked them to change the tyres. Then, feeling like a lamb going to the slaughter, I was ushered off by Tex to learn some of the essential circus skills I would need for tomorrow.

Rope spinning . . . Ha! How difficult can it be to spin a bit of old twine above your head like Roy Rogers? Then, inside the Big Top, it struck me that Nicky (the director), Tex and Julie, as well as everyone else at Jay Miller's were expecting me to entertain the crowds the next day. Now was clearly not the time to be flippant about rope spinning.

Tex began by showing me how he got the momentum of the rope going in the right way, then encouraged me to have a go. 'Stand clear, folks, this could be messy,' I declared, as I struggled to get the rope up over my head while it was still turning – it was going to be much more difficult than I'd thought.

'It took me six months to learn how to do this properly,' said Julie. She had been invited to join a circus by her brother, who had been the general maintenance man. Having worked in a factory after leaving school, then trying her hand at hairdressing and nursing, she had decided that the nomadic, low-paid life of a circus performer was for her. How was little old me going to be able to spin a rope in two days, when it had taken Julie six months to perfect? Good question!

The Los Alexandros act involved scenes set in a saloon in the old American West, cowboy country, and in addition to rope spinning, which was a major part of the ten-minute piece, Tex tore up pieces of newspaper with horse whips and, of course, threw knives at Julie while she stood against a board. I *had* to try to master the art of rope spinning, so that I didn't let Tex and Julie down, but I felt an overwhelming urge to pack my trunk and say goodbye to the circus, like poor old Nelly the Elephant. I'm a real trouper, though, so I decided to trudge onwards and upwards and took my rope off to a quiet corner of the Big Top to practise, away from prying eyes. Fat lot of good it did me, though: several Russian women, busy teaching their children to do the splits, took time out to have a good old chuckle at me.

The people around me were all completely dedicated to the life of the circus. Take Mike the ringmaster, for example. Until about ten years ago he'd been a manager with a large insurance company, then suddenly decided to join the circus. Why? What was it about a circus career that appealed to him and everyone else here? Living in a caravan for nine months of the year, without a single day off and earning between £70 and £120 a week wasn't my idea of a worker's paradise. But as Tex and Julie said, 'Circus life isn't financially rewarding and it can be stressful, but when you stand in the ring twice a day entertaining the crowds you get a real buzz at seeing people laugh and enjoy themselves. The fact that we move from place to place doesn't give us time to get bored with our surroundings. There are no real social pressures here – the next-door neighbours do the same job – and there's a real sense of family, even though many of the performers are from Eastern Europe and barely speak English. The tradition of the circus is another big plus. There's something very romantic about being in it, and we love it. This really is a way of life, not simply a job. The moment you look at it as a job, you really ought to consider giving up!'

Before you ask, no, I wasn't about to give up, I still had to master my ridiculous bit of rope and, no doubt, one or two other skills.

Tex discovered me in my corner, like a small child hiding from the schoolmaster. 'Julie needs you back in the van, please, mate,' he said. I left my new guide and mentor to connect up his cables to the generator, and headed back across the racecourse to the Alexandros ranch.

'Excellent, Jeremy, you've arrived just at the right time. See those sequins there? Well, they need sewing on to that waistcoat.' Julie, it transpired, was charged with the task of making all the costumes for the act, which filled what little spare time she had. 'Some of the costumes can take me up to two months to finish, and with being pregnant I'm having to let most of mine out to accommodate the increase in my waist size.' I promptly informed her that this might be handy, given that my own girth was felt by some to be considerable. 'One small snag, though, Jeremy. You'll have to wear the dresses!' Julie told me.

Great! Not only was I going to have to stand in the ring performing miracles with a piece of twine, I'd also have to wear one of Julie's spangly frocks! Could this get any worse? Possibly!

While I'd been discussing with Julie the finer points of trying to live in the two fairly cramped rooms of a caravan – which would prove a real challenge to the best of us – Tex had been busy preparing the next element of my training. 'Right then, Jeremy, let's see how good you are with knives,' he said with a smirk, as he entered the caravan.

'Well, I can peel a potato, whittle wood and cut up meat. Why?' was my cheeky reply.

'That's not exactly what I had in mind. I want you to practise throwing these.' Tex was in the process of passing me some long steel blades, whose handles were wrapped in bits of sequined fabric.

'Hey up! Julie's been at your kitchen knives, an' all, Tex.'

He wasn't amused. 'Come on, calm down,' he said, 'this is a serious business. You need to demonstrate an ability to handle these knives if I'm going to be able to throw them at you tomorrow.'

'Wait one cotton-pickin' minute, bud!' was my immediate response, in a pseudo-Deep South American accent. 'Did I hear ya right, boy? Did y'all say you was gonna chuck those there little shiny things at me, boy?' Hoping I'd misheard him, I laughed nervously – yes, you're right, it's becoming a bit of a tradition for me with this series: every time I get pushed towards the edge of toughness, I have no choice but to laugh.

Sadly for me, my hearing hadn't failed me and I found myself clutching the knives and standing about four feet away from a large wooden board, which had been decorated with wooden playing cards. This was the board against which Tex intended me to stand for him to throw *knives* at me! As you might expect, I'd begun to sweat quite a bit at the thought of this.

'Now, Jeremy, as with everything in the circus, there is a definite technique for you to learn.' Tex was trying desperately to get me to focus on the job in hand. 'It's as easy as that,' he tossed one to demonstrate, 'but, remember, it's not all in the wrist but the entire method from start to end.'

While I was happy to have a go at throwing the knives at the board, I was less than enamoured with the idea of being his victim.

As with the rope, my knife-throwing expertise clearly needed brushing up. Tex generously agreed to give me a bit of time to become acquainted with the blades. How kind of him, don't you think?

I needed to find a way to stall him so that I wouldn't have to stand in front of the board and face death in the name of television excellence. I persuaded him to chat about his life: 'I've known nothing but the circus. My dad taught me every-thing, so it's very difficult for me to consider doing anything else to earn a living.' He explained that in the winter months, when the circus is not on tour, he and Julie, like almost all other circus performers, have to find part-time work to keep the wolves at bay. Tex holds an HGV licence and generally drives lorries – he claimed he enjoyed this as much as performing, but although he demonstrated a passion for British ERF trucks, his first love was clearly the circus. His father, I discovered, had died in Tex's arms, when Tex was fifteen, from a heart-attack while performing in the ring. Tex's Italian/Spanish mother made him get back into the ring almost straight away and continue his dad's act. It was clear why he was so committed to this lifestyle.

Julie, from what I could see, was simply fascinated by the whole business of the circus, and there was a sparkle in her eye when she spoke of the act. Maybe it was being able to escape for ten minutes twice a day to become a cowgirl that kept her in the ring.

Before I had had a chance to catch my breath, I was whisked into the Big Top to watch the first of the day's performances. 'This will give you a chance to see how the act works, and where you and and Tex will need to be,' explained Julie, who was wearing a rather fetching red usher's uniform. 'I'll leave you here right at the front of the stalls. That way you'll be able to experience the act right up close, Jeremy! I need to whiz off now and help Ludmilla [a charming woman from Moldova] to sell the popcorn, sweets, drinks and merchandise,' and with that Julie sped off. This was a small circus where everyone was expected to turn their hand to anything that needed doing. It was clear that a real sense of team spirit existed among the performers. It felt almost like a commune where everyone looked out for everyone else. They all did at least three jobs to keep the circus ticking over, which was great if you wanted to be busy all day, but not if you were in need of a siesta.

The auditorium was about three-quarters full, and the kids were all harassing their parents, grandparents and friends to fork out for candy-floss, popcorn and ice-cream, so poor Julie was being run ragged. I sat looking around the Big Top still trying to get to grips with the draw of circus life. Then I found myself trying to imagine what it was like back in the 1820s when tents – and, yes, I am allowed to say tents here – were first used. Had life changed much for the performer since then? Sure, the acts had improved and become more technical, and the tents had turned into Big Tops, but the performers were still having to live the life of nomads traipsing far and wide to earn a few bob. Incredible!

My daydreaming came to an abrupt end as ringmaster Mike picked up his microphone and bellowed out a few details about the forthcoming performance. Much excitement filled the Big Top, and I found myself feeling even more pressured than before – after all, it was going to be me in that ring tomorrow trying to generate excitement in the crowd. Oh, Lord, I still hadn't had any knives thrown at me – and as for that blessed rope, well, I had a long way to go before I could spin the damn thing like Roy Rogers.

The show continued apace, and included Hungarian jugglers, Ukrainian gymnasts, Moldovan high-wire performers, a British clown and, of course, Los Alexandros. As Tex and Julie emerged into the ring, resplendent in their Wild West costumes, they set about a rapid succession of tricks, involving cards, ropes, whips and, yes, those huge great blades! I was getting to grips with what was expected of me the next day, and beginning to feel more relaxed and, dare I say it?, confident that I could bluff my way through the show.

That is, until I felt the heat of a naked flame enter the ring. Why had Volodya, one of the assistants, come in clutching a set of knives that were on fire? Yes, on FIRE! Surely, Tex wasn't going to throw those at Julie? Because if he was, there was a strong chance he'd be tossing them in my direction tomorrow evening. Oh, for sure! I could barely bring myself to open my eyes to see the flames spin through the air towards Julie, who appeared amazingly calm. Tex was throwing these things around as though they were cotton buds – you know, those plastic stick things with a bit of cotton wool at either end. This was surely going to end in misery.

Thankfully, the rest of the performance passed without incident, but I wasn't feeling any happier about the flames. 'Tex, are you planning to toss flaming blades at me tomorrow?' I asked anxiously after the show had finished.

'Probab—'

Julie stepped in: 'I doubt it, Jeremy, but we'll talk you through the whole act early tomorrow morning. Then we can fine-tune how we'll all work the shows tomorrow.'

My nervous system began to calm, and I left my mentor and his assistant to prepare for the second show of the day. In case you're wondering, there's a show at five o'clock and another at seven, and I needed all the sleep I could get if I was going to get through the traumas of both tomorrow.

There was, however, one consolation as I nodded off to sleep in my hotel room – sorry, I couldn't bring myself to sleep the night in a breezy caravan: some things are above and beyond the call of duty. At least I wasn't going to have to join Oleg as his flying-trapeze assistant. Here's another piece of circus information for you: the trapeze became an integral part of the modern circus sometime during 1859, when it was invented by some madman who clearly had taken leave of his senses.

Anyway, enough of that, you'll be amazed to hear that I had the most wonderful night's sleep, not once dreaming of death by Tex's flaming blades. As I sat eating my breakfast the following morning, however, Simon, the ever-cheery cameraman, reminded me that I still had to master the rope, the whips and, of course, the knives. 'Thanks, Simon. I think it's time to go back to bed and catch up on some of the sleep deprivation I've suffered of late.' But Nicky bundled me straight into the car and we rushed back to the circus.

Tex and Julie were, I'm sorry to report, on top form, which meant I was in for a busy day getting to grips with the evening's entertainment. We discussed the act over a cup of coffee and it was decided, much to my relief, that I wouldn't have to face the flaming knives. 'Ah, but if you think you're getting out of it that easily, you're mistaken, Jeremy,' declared Tex and Julie simultaneously.

'You come with us to the Big Top and we'll have you cracking whips, spinning ropes and, of course, facing the knives with your eyes open before five o'clock,' said Julie. And neither of them was joking. This was a serious business, and their reputations were resting on my shoulders. I needed to shape up or ship out. What a choice!

Never one to shirk my responsibilities, I stood in front of the knife board feeling like an uncut loaf about to be sliced into thick and thin pieces. Julie positioned me in exactly the right spot, as Tex raised his arm in preparation. 'Ooh, be careful, I'm a little bit wider than Julie, and a tad taller – you will take that into consideration as you hurl those at me, won't you?' came my desperate plea to my mentor.

Tex hadn't even started to answer before I felt the cold rush of air as a blade sped past me towards the board. In the blink of an eye – at least I think I had them open in order for them to blink – it was over. Eight blades, or thereabouts – who was counting at this stage? – had struck the board without incident. Now seemed the perfect moment for me to ask Julie, 'Has he ever hit or injured you with these little beauties?'

'Only once,' she proclaimed.

'Once! Excuse me, I'm quitting while I'm ahead, if you don't mind. My mum always told me never to tempt Fate.' Julie went on to explain that she had once made a costume with incredibly large sleeves, which one of Tex's knives had caught, pinning her to the board. She tried to reassure me that no blood was drawn, but for some reason my brain was telling me not to trust my travelling friends.

Late that morning I went on to crack a whip with great accuracy but, alas, the rope spinning was still evading me. I was determined, however, to give it a whirl on the night.

My watch seemed to be travelling at an incredible speed that day, and I found myself donning my performer's costume much sooner than I had hoped. In a pair of black trousers and white shirt topped off with a rather fetching gold Stetson and waistcoat, I stood behind the ring with my new colleagues waiting for the curtain to go up. Now, I've worked in a theatre before and know how it feels to wait for a show to start, but this was something different. I had absolutely no idea how to spin a rope, and wasn't too keen on knives being thrown at me but, hell, that's show business.

Then Mike the ringmaster was talking: 'Introducing Los Alexandros and their special star performer – Jeremy Spake.'

'Mike, don't go telling people I'm here!' But it was too late. He looked at me with a knowing smile, which said, 'Get a life and get out there, knock them dead, and feel the thrill of the circus.'

The performance was a triumph, even if I say so myself. Okay, the rope was a disaster, but I cleverly pulled a member of the audience into the ring to have a go with it, thus demonstrating to the crowd just how hard it was. I even managed to keep my underwear clean during the knife throwing. Tex and Julie were delighted with my performance, and were happy for me to join them for the second show. Funnily enough, I found myself really getting into it the second time round, to the extent that I was using my rather pathetic American accent on the public, who appeared to love every minute of it.

After the show, I asked some of the audience, 'Would you like to be a circus performer?'

Most of them replied, 'Yes – travelling round and enjoying yourself, what could be better?' Did they have any perception of what really goes on in a circus? Probably not, because if they had they would have realized that the actual performances are a very small part of what being a circus performer is all about. It struck me that this might be quite a lonely life – after all, how often did Tex and Julie get the chance to catch up with their relatives and friends back home in the Midlands? Hardly ever. How often did they get a day off? Hardly ever. How often could they spend money on the occasional little luxury? Almost never. The circus is one of those professions that is a vocation and not simply a job. The people who choose this way of life probably don't consider it tough, but I found just two days of it pretty exhausting, but nevertheless enjoyable.

Would *I* want to join the circus permanently? I think I'll leave it to the wonderful professionals: I'd much prefer to sit and watch, although I'll probably never look at it in the same way ever again.

# chapter five
# HILL
# FARMER

***Salary:*** Virtually nothing, although a figure of between £3.73 and
£4.89 per hour has been suggested by government sources.

***Requirements:*** Only strong, physically fit people who love
working outside year-round need apply. Applicants should
appreciate that there is little money in farming, and that they will
be doing it for love and not financial reward. (It should be noted
that our visit to the farm was made before the outbreak of the
foot-and-mouth crisis in the summer of 2001.)

***Toughness rating:*** 14

**C**an you imagine my excitement when Zoë in the
production office informed me, 'You're off to
Bethlehem next week, Jeremy! I'll get the call sheet off to
you as soon as I can.' She had made my day! At last a
*Toughest Job* venue in the sun – Bethlehem, the Holy Land!
Like all good travellers I immediately dashed out to buy my

suntan lotion – after all, you don't want to get burnt while you're filming, do you?

But don't bother imagining my excitement. Try picturing my face when, three days later, I switched on my computer to find an e-mail from the gorgeous Zoë, with the keenly anticipated call sheet attached. With great enthusiasm I downloaded the magical document, and shut my office door so that I could savour the moment. The warm sea, good food and, above all, the sun! Marvellous!

Hang on a minute – what's this written here? Catch a train to Cardiff? Sorry, shouldn't I be going to Heathrow to catch a plane? The simple answer to this was . . . NO!

My instructions were clear: I needed to get myself to Cardiff, where I would be met by Leceia, my researcher, and driven to Bethlehem in the Brecon Beacons – Wales! Great! Not that I've got anything against Wales – in fact, I love the Brecons, but when you've pictured yourself in the Holy Land getting a tan, it's not quite the same thing now, is it?

As I stepped off the train, in true British fashion the heavens opened. It was April, and clearly I wasn't going to be needing my suntan lotion! What did the next two days hold in store for me in the Brecon Beacons – which I might add are used by the élite forces of the British Army to train their personnel to survive in harsh conditions? 'Leceia, honeychild, what exactly are we going to be filming here?'

Without batting an eyelid, my researcher responded, 'What else would you film in Bethlehem but a shepherd?'

I was beginning to feel like I was about to become the victim of something like *Candid Camera*, or the famous Noel Edmonds 'Gotcha' Oscar. 'Are you being serious?' seemed like a good question to ask at the time.

She did not respond, except to hand me a briefing document on Nick and Kyra Somerfield.

Sure enough, as I read a little bit about Nick and Kyra, I discovered I would be working alongside an English couple who had been shepherds on the same farm in Wales for more than thirty-seven years. The document also explained that it was lambing season, and that they had more than three hundred sheep in their flock. I was going to be a very busy chap indeed.

After a short but comfortable night's sleep in a hotel about five miles from Bethlehem, I found myself knocking on the door of the Crug-las farmhouse as the sun was rising at six-thirty a.m. A fairly tall, slim, somewhat dishevelled figure emerged from behind the door, with an enormous grin on his face, and a voice as powerful as mine. 'Jeremy, good to meet you! You've arrived on the farm at exactly the right time. There's plenty to do, but first come in and meet Kyra.' Nick struck me as a really likeable character, with boundless energy, which, given that he was about thirty years my senior, was worrying to say the least.

Having wrestled off my wellington boots, I followed him into the kitchen. Kyra, who had a most welcoming smile, was standing by the Aga feeding a tiny lamb with a baby's bottle. Everything felt right. This was definitely how I had pictured the farm and its owners. 'Kyra, it's great to meet you! Who's this here, then?'

As Kyra answered my question, it was apparent that she was one formidable lady, who was dedicated to farming: 'This is Tarzan, and down there is Jane.' Kyra was gesturing at another tiny lamb, who had been placed in a home-made pen next to the cooker on the kitchen floor. 'Both of them were left for dead yesterday by their mothers. We've been nursing them ever since.' It transpired that it was quite normal to discover Nick and Kyra's kitchen looking like a scene from *Dr Doolittle*, and that almost every lambing season they ended up with abandoned runts living there, in the hope that they could keep them alive and strengthen them up to join the rest of the flock on the hillside.

Over Tarzan's bleating – believe me, he could bleat for the entire flock – Nick explained what he hoped we could achieve over the two days I would be on the farm. 'It's great to have an extra pair of hands, Jeremy. There's so much that needs seeing to. We'll start with inoculating Kyra's goats, if that's all right.'

That seemed to me as good a place to start as any, but what did I know about farming – let alone where to begin?

As we stepped out into the daylight, I had my first chance to look around at the scenery that surrounded the slightly ramshackle but cheerful farm. This family business nestles on the edge of the Brecon Beacons, which is certainly an area of outstanding natural beauty, and since 1957 has been classified as a National Park. Nick explained to me that the European Union categorized the land on which the farm stood as 'with severe difficulty of terrain, altitude or climatic conditions'. 'Dare I ask exactly what they mean by that?' Quite why I asked this question I don't really know: the answer was staring me in the face.

'It's impossible to grow any crops on this land, so all you can do is farm livestock. The weather conditions here are harsh, and there are the fighters from the RAF base along the road, which over-fly low enough for you to see whether or not the pilot has had a shave today. All of this, and the fact that the farm is situated on the edge of one of Britain's National Parks, makes farming tricky.'

I had a feeling I was going to discover for myself just how difficult it was to be a hill farmer in this part of the world.

I found Denis, Paul and Stuart, the camera crew, standing with Kyra in a small single-storey stable adjacent to the farmhouse. My arrival was hailed by a chorus of bleating goats, who seemed less than happy to see Nick and me clutching the inoculation kit. As part of her commitment to farming, Kyra had spent the past fifteen years supporting Farm Africa, a charitable group who assist with farming projects throughout Africa. She has been breeding pedigree British Toggenburg goats for seven years in connection with the Farm Africa Charity aid programme to Ethiopia. Kyra's contribution is helping less fortunate Ethiopian farmers cope with the arid and harsh conditions that surround them. This was amazing, given that Kyra was already struggling to prevent hers and Nick's farm being turned into another holiday home for tourists.

How tricky can it be to catch a goat in a pen that measures approximately eight feet by five? Nigh on impossible when there are five or six of the little bleaters all ganging up on you. I was beginning to regret not having taken some animal-handling tips from my old mate Trude Mostue of *Vets in Practice* fame. The sight of my large frame scurrying around the stable in pursuit of the pedigree perishers must have been something to behold, and Denis certainly had the odd laugh at my expense. Thankfully, though, Nick came to my rescue as I fell to the floor for the third time in less than two minutes. 'These are pretty meaty goats, Kyra,' I proclaimed, as I tried to hold one still in my arms while Kyra inoculated it against a whole batch of potentially nasty things.

'The great thing about this breed is that they're tough, very dairy productive and can survive and thrive in the harsh conditions here as well as in Africa.' Kyra's passion for them was obvious, but I fear Nick was less than enamoured with them as they continued to give him the slip in the pen behind us.

The director John and Leceia had already visited the farm and chatted with Nick and Kyra about the format of the show, so they were well aware of the need to keep me busy to demonstrate how tough things were.

Little did I know that they would take the production staff's words so literally. Having exhausted myself trying to catch goats, I had a shovel thrust in my hand. What followed? Well, Nick informed me, 'We need to go into the cowshed over there, Jeremy, and clear out some of the muck.'

In addition to the 320 or so Welsh mountain ewes and endless lambs, the handful of Texel rams and couple of sheepdogs, there were approximately sixty-five head of cattle, who were calving during my visit. Needless to say, this number of animals meant there was an awful lot of muck. As Nick and I got to grips with what seemed like a ton of pure cowpat in the shed, I asked, 'What about your sons, Nick? Don't they work with you?' Nick, who is the chairman of the 'Land Use' Parliamentary Committee for the Farmers Union of Wales that advises the Welsh Assembly, is only too aware of the stresses of modern farming. 'We simply cannot generate enough income here to sustain us and the boys, who all have families. Ten years ago we were getting something in the region of thirty to forty pounds a lamb, depending on size, but today we're lucky if a lamb fetches more than twenty.' This, I felt, was horrifying given the cost-of-living increases that had occurred in ten years. Perhaps the main cause of this decline in stock values for farmers is the large-scale importing of foreign lamb. Unlike in other parts of the world, the Welsh lambing season takes place only once a year and lasts for a short period of time, which, as I am sure you can appreciate, increases the pressure on farmers like Nick and Kyra. Nick explained that while his three sons would dearly have loved to farm, they simply couldn't let their families starve, and had ended up working as a carpenter, a stone mason and a marine engineer. I now understood why the farm looked loved, and very much lived in: Nick and Kyra couldn't afford to pay anyone to assist them and were struggling from day to day to get the essential jobs done.

It was clear that, while I wasn't much good at farming, I was going to be able to offer some real help during my time at Crug-las. So, without so much as a groan – after all, I didn't have to spend 365 days of the year tethered to an ailing farm trying to keep my head above water – I dug in and helped Nick fill a mechanical muck-spreader. The cow-poo was flying all over the place as I tossed it through the door into the trailer outside. Denis was slowly getting covered and, without realizing it, I'd managed to cake the camera lens in huge clods of freshly laid muck. Fantastic!

Before we set off up the hillside to conduct one of five or six daily checks on the flock, Kyra invited us all into the kitchen for lunch. Tarzan, who was still bleating for Britain, was just as hungry as the rest of us. Still wearing her coat, Kyra was stirring our soup at the same time as she fed Tarzan. He was a handsome little Welsh mountain lamb, and I have to confess I adopted him, but more of that later.

'Right, Jeremy, this is the newest piece of equipment we have here,' said Nick, with a certain sense of achievement in his voice. What stood before me was a green quad bike, which appeared to be about seven years old.

One glance across the farmyard revealed that Nick wasn't kidding: most of his tractors – which, much to my delight, were of East European origin – were all looking pretty sorry for themselves. Kyra laughed as I enquired, 'How much would a new tractor set you back, folks?'

'We don't talk about such things here,' Nick said, in his usual light-hearted way. '"New" and "equipment" are words that simply don't go together in this part of the world, I'm afraid.'

Then we were off, thundering up the hill like something from the Charge of the Light Brigade at Balaclava. Nick doesn't hang around. I'd hopped into a small trailer, which had been hooked up to the quad bike, and was being thrown all over the place as he wrestled with the muddy terrain below the wheels. He was in his element: he looked like a kid with a new toy. 'It's great, this thing, Jeremy,' he said. 'It enables me to cover virtually the whole farm in a quarter of the time it used to take me on foot.' I couldn't imagine how long it took on foot: 220 acres is a fair patch to have to cover several times a day, wouldn't you agree?

I forgot to mention that on the way up the hill poor old Denis, who had squashed into the trailer with me and Paul to film, had been thrust against the trailer gate, which sprang open, leaving my favourite cameraman stuck on his bum in the mud. For a change it wasn't me in the embarrassing position of legs akimbo. 'Denis, you ought to hold on tight, mate!'

'Very funny, Jeremy. My hands are freezing, and it's pretty difficult to hold on tight while filming!'

I decided to extend my arm and assist him to his feet, rather than risk a tongue-lashing from my old comrade.

Once at the top of the hill we had a commanding view of the surrounding stunning countryside. 'Kyra and I are delighted to be looking after this land for future generations, despite the struggle,' Nick said.

This statement fascinated me. 'But you're the landowners here. Aren't you going to pass it on to your children?' I asked.

'Well, we're merely the custodians of it for the generation of people who come here after us, and they probably won't be my family,' Nick replied.

It was clear to me already that Nick and Kyra had more or less worked out exactly what life meant to them, and what role they had to play during their lives. In our ever-crazy high-tech world, most of us crave bigger and better, which has made many of us fairly selfish. Let's face it, if Mrs Jones next door has the very latest video/DVD player in her living room, Mrs Smith has simply got to go out and buy it too. By the way, if your name is Smith or Jones, please don't think I'm picking on you: I'm simply using this well-known phrase as an illustration of how things often appear! Other people, however, like Nick and Kyra, don't worry about the everyday trappings of modern living, and feel it is their mission to try to leave something tangible for those who will inherit the planet from us. This, I think, is a rare quality, and I liked my new farming friends more and more.

Our third trip up the hill showed us why Nick had to make regular visits to check on the flock: a two-day-old lamb had wandered through a barbed-wire fence and fallen into a shallow ditch. Unfortunately, it was unable to get itself out of its predicament, and its distressed mother stood helplessly looking on. Nick leapt out of the trailer – he had allowed me to drive up the hill, which I thought was a much safer bet for Denis and the rest of us – and jumped into the ditch. Please bear in mind, folks, that this man is over sixty, and made me feel like the couch potato that I am – very embarrassing, I can assure you. 'Right, Jeremy, I'll pass you this escapee to put over there near Mum.'

As I took hold of the lamb and had a bit of a cuddle – sorry, I'm a great big softie at heart – I began to enjoy life as a shepherd. I put Larry – he had to be called Larry after the famous lamb – back on the ground and said, 'Go on, off you go. Go to Mum!'

Nick was chuckling to himself – he could see how I was becoming hooked on the job, which was certainly tough but seemed immensely rewarding to me.

I was enjoying myself so much that I hadn't even noticed how late it was. The day had sped past and it was time to say goodnight to Crug-las and head for my hotel. Still, it had been a packed sixteen-hour day, and I'd had so much fresh air I was truly knackered.

Day two started, as you might expect, at the wonderful time of six a.m., but I couldn't get to the farm soon enough.

John, the director, seemed slightly put out that I was enjoying myself so much. It's hard for the directors, who have to ensure that I endure every last moment of toughness each job can have, but this was one where it didn't matter to me how difficult it got. Which was a good thing, really.

Nick greeted me in his usual effervescent manner: 'Morning, Jeremy! I do hope you've slept well, because I'm going to be needing you to have as much strength as possible today. I was up at three a.m. with a cow in distress giving birth and I'm feeling a bit tired.'

Typical! There I'd been in my bed, fast asleep counting sheep, and Nick had been dealing with a trauma on the farm that to him probably seemed routine but to us would have been a major event. As he explained what had happened, John was looking decidedly fed up. You have to remember that it's important for us to give a true picture to the audience of every aspect of a given job, and if being up at three a.m. is part of it, we should have been there. I think all of us were kicking ourselves that we hadn't stayed at the farm. Still, life goes on, and Nick needed me to go and do the first checks of the day up on the hillside.

As I sped off on the quad bike, I spotted the eldest of the Somerfield boys – the marine engineer – building a new hay trailer out of cannibalized parts, and decided to have a quick chat with him about his parents. 'They're amazing,' he said, 'they've dedicated thirty-seven years to this place. I'd love to be here with them, especially as it's getting too much for them both. Sadly, though, the farm can't make enough money to feed us all.' I knew from my chats with both Nick and Kyra that they were sad their offspring couldn't be a part of everyday life on the farm.

My trip round the farm was uneventful, which was a great relief. When I got back to the farmyard, which was now almost free of cow-poo because we'd loaded most of it into the muck-spreader the day before, I found Nick hitching up his newly finished trailer to his ancient Czech-built tractor. 'Jeremy,' he said, 'we need to pop about three miles up the road to a neighbour's farm where I store my cattle feed.' No sooner had he finished speaking than we were off.

As we loaded the large bales of rolled feed – they're those big black plastic-covered things you often see in fields in the country – disaster struck. 'Nick, that tyre looks a bit flat to me.'

Nick descended from the tractor's cab. 'Sod it, I should have put a bit of air in those tyres before we left the farm!' Nice one, Nick! Just when things were going well, we've got a minor catastrophe on our hands.

What was all the fuss about? I hear you ask.

Simple, we'd already loaded three bales on to the blessed trailer, and they were wedged, so removing them, so that we could blow up the tyres, without the assistance of another piece of farm equipment was going to be tricky. I borrowed the BBC production vehicle and ran Nick back up the hill to the farm, where he introduced me to another item in his antiquated armoury. This time it was a prehistoric air pressure pump and hose, connected up to an equally ancient Land Rover. Both sprang to life, however, and we sped off back down the hill to get the trailer moving again.

Having overcome this little challenge, in true Nick style with smiles on our faces, it was time to pop into town to pay a few bills and buy some wire fencing and posts from the local farmers' supply store.

On our way to the bank Nick was telling me about how he'd ended up in Bethlehem: 'Well, you see, having left agricultural college, Kyra – who, by the way, was my childhood sweetheart – and I wanted to buy a farm but couldn't afford one anywhere in England. We eventually managed to persuade the bank to give us a mortgage and bought Crug-las.' I was amazed to hear that they still owed on their mort-gage thirty-seven years later! That's tough!

'What keeps you both going?' I asked.

'Well, farming is still a vital part of life in Britain, and although as a profession we have probably the highest suicide rate, it's very rewarding to be making your contribu-tion to the national economy at such a basic and fundamen-tal level. I've never been one for those computer gadgets.' Once again Nick had made sense and demonstrated his grip on reality. He was one boss for whom I could happily have worked. As we drove back to Bethlehem, having procured all we needed to repair a damaged fence, we shared our opin-ions on the world and its politics, discovering that we were indeed kindred spirits.

Back at the farm Nick invited me, under his supervision, to have a go at tractor driving. There was no need for him to ask twice; I jumped at the chance and hopped into the cab. The crew followed us to a field where I was going to be spreading some of the wonderfully fresh muck we'd collected the day before. Much to my amusement Denis and the boys had insisted I drive well clear of them as they filmed Nick and me working. Need you ask? This was like a red rag to a bull. 'Oh, boys, please!' I said. 'Don't worry, I'll steer well clear of you all. I don't want you getting all dirty and smelly, now, do I?' I charged past them as close as I dared, and on the return leg caught sight of my splattered colleagues. Nick and I chuckled all the way back to the farm as the boys frantically turned the production vehicle upside down looking for wet wipes!!

Kyra, who'd been busy looking after the goats, cows and odd stray sheep down in the farmyard, was pleased to see us return. It was three o'clock and time for a rather late lunch. She was eager for me to catch up with Tarzan too. As we tucked into doorstep wedges of bread and cheese, I asked her, 'What will happen to Tarzan?' I'll take this opportunity to remind you that he'd already cheated death two nights earlier.

'Because he's a bit of a runt, we'd be lucky to sell him, so he'll be another of the farm pets, no doubt. If we can't afford to keep him as a pet, we'll have to put him to sleep.'

'If you did try to sell him, how much do you think you'd get?' I asked.

'About ten pounds, if we're really lucky.'

This seemed sad: having survived, this poor little mite was now worth next to nothing to my struggling farming friends who, at the end of the day, were running a business. At this point I said nothing more, but I was already plotting with the crew for us all to make a donation towards Tarzan's upkeep so that they could keep him as their BBC pet sheep. In fact, the following day, as we were leaving the area to return to London, Leceia, John and I returned to the farm to hand over sixty pounds towards his first year's board and lodging. We have subsequently sent more donations and Tarzan now rules the roost, making a nuisance of himself every day. He's a formidable force on the Somerfield holding.

'Jeremy, can you give me a hand with the fence before the light goes?' Nick asked, then yawned.

'And just before you go, take a look at this list I've prepared for you'. Kyra handed me a scrap of paper, upon which she had noted some of the skills she felt a good farmer needed. The list went something like this: engineer, driver, herdsman, vet, biologist, chemist, botanist, builder, labourer, mechanic, salesman . . . it went on and on. She had shown me that farming was not simple.

I cut my hands a few times while I was helping Nick run long lines of barbed wire along a row of posts we'd bashed into the ground, but as we worked I asked him how much time he and Kyra had spent away from the farm. 'The only real time I've ever spent away from here was when I fell off one of the barn roofs and ended up in hospital. They wanted me to stay in for a few days to monitor my condition. With it being lambing season I hadn't got time to sit feeling sorry for myself so I discharged myself pretty *tout de suite.*'

This seemed like madness to me – but needs must. 'Was that the only time you've been away?' I asked, wondering when they had holidays.

'Oh, the kids paid for us to go to Paris for our anniversary not so long ago, which was nice, but we both spent the time worrying about the farm, so didn't relax very much.'

I thought, Lordy Lord, this farming lark needs a full-on commitment.

Sadly, my time as a shepherd in Bethlehem had come to an end. As we sat eating supper, Nick and Kyra announced that they wanted to share their earnings with me for all the hard work I had done over the thirty-four hours I'd worked on the farm.

'There's no need, honestly, it's been a pleasure,' I said.

'No, no, we insist.' They handed me my pay packet and reminded me that this was my share of our earnings.

'How much? *Six pounds forty-three!* Is this really all I earned?'

'Well, it's certainly all we can afford to pay.' Given that the Government has stipulated a minimum wage of £3.73 per hour for casual workers, it struck me as incredible, but clearly demonstrated how hard life was for them.

I left feeling nothing but admiration for Nick and Kyra, and, indeed, at the end of the series, decided that they had the Toughest Job. I still keep in regular contact with them, and receive updates on Tarzan's progress. There can be no doubt that hill farming continues to be tough.

# chapter six
# HOLIDAY
# REP

**Salary:** Approximately £7000 per annum; accommodation, meals and expenses provided by the company.

**Requirements:** Applicants should have the ability to work long hours, be diplomatic, caring and cheerful even in the face of adversity. Above all, they must be gregarious and like people.

### Toughness rating: 9

Receiving post is an ordinary occurrence for most of us, but receiving post from the production office of a show like *Toughest Job in Britain* is anything but ordinary, I can assure you. Taking into account the nature of the programme, those large brown envelopes sent from the office can mean only one thing – TROUBLE! I'm sure you are beginning to appreciate this as you delve further into the pages of this book. As I opened one particular envelope, terrifyingly marked BBC, you cannot imagine my surprise at learning the topic of my next Tough Job. Written at the top of my call sheet – the document explaining about the next film – were the words 'Overseas Holiday Rep'.

At last! An opportunity to use the copious amounts of suntan lotion I'd purchased for my trip to Bethlehem, the Holy Land, which turned out to be Bethlehem, Wales. Finally, someone had decided to let me take it easy. The sun, sand and delights of an overseas trip! As is often the case with this series, my mind was running wild, and as I read my call sheet with great excitement I conjured up visions of lying on the beach all day, only having to deal with the occasional disgruntled Brit. Heaven! I'm a past master at dealing with unhappy customers! Where were they sending me to top up on my non-existent tan? I was heading for . . . Tenerife, one of the most popular holiday destinations with the British.

Tenerife, for those of you who've never been there, is the largest of the Spanish Canary Islands, and lies off the northwest coast of Africa. The island itself is approximately sixty miles long and at its broadest point is approximately thirty miles wide. Most of it is occupied by a volcanic mountain called Pico de Teide, which rises to 12,188 feet at its peak. The name 'Tenerife', in Guanche, a local dialect, means 'snow-capped mountain'. Although tourism is the main source of income to the island, and the reason I was sent there, it produces a number of agricultural crops including dates, bananas, other fruits, maize, sugar and tomatoes. Believe it or not, Francisco Franco and his supporters planned the Nationalist rebellion in Tenerife in 1936, which led to the Spanish Civil War. Today the island is home to nearly 800,000 inhabitants, and plays host to hundreds of thousands of tourists from all over the world every year.

After the usual delays at Gatwick – well, let's face it, a holiday wouldn't be the same without having a bit of an air-traffic-control delay, now, would it? – we had a nice smooth four-hour flight to the southern tip of this popular holiday haunt. I spent most of the flight chatting with the cabin crew – now there's a surprise! And just before landing, as you might expect, I wangled a seat on the flight deck and chinwagged with the pilots as we made our approach. The weather was fantastic, just a light south-westerly breeze, and, of course, the sun was doing what it does best – shining! Oh, just how tough could this possibly be? I asked myself.

As I stood with my team at the baggage carousel, Alison, the film's researcher, began to give me some more information concerning the main character we would be following. 'Jeremy, you'll need to find Paul Mobbs, who's thirty, larger than life, and waiting for us just the other side of those doors.'

'OK,' rolled off my tongue. All this sounded great, a chap similar in age to my good self, and larger than life, which always bodes well with me. What I didn't appreciate was that Paul looks after all the holidaymakers between the ages of eighteen and thirty.

When I met Paul, who had been working since 1996 in Tenerife as a Club Freestyle rep for Thomson Holidays – one of the world's largest tour operators, selling more than four million package tours annually – it was immediately obvious why he was looking after the young party-going jet-setters. He was, in his own words, 'Givin' it large!' 'You see, Jeremy, it's really important to keep the energy going all the time, and make sure you're always givin' it large to the kids. They're relying on us to make their holidays for them!' Great. I've been filming non-stop for nearly four months without any time off and now, instead of being able to lie on a beach catching some rays, I was going to be running around nursing a load of eighteen-year-olds, who really ought to know how to have fun without my help anyway!

There was, however, one saving grace. My team and I were not going to be staying in the same hotel as the party animals. Oh, no! We'd been booked into a very nice hotel some twenty minutes west of Playa de las Americas, the main resort in the south of the island where all of the teenagers were staying. Was I pleased about this? You're not kidding I was, especially if the coach trip into Playa to drop off the new young arrivals was anything to go by. Most of the blokes had enjoyed the odd beer or two on the plane, and were ready for anything. All I wanted to do was go to bed! Sad, I know, but I'd been feeling like I'd reached pensionable age since touching down at the airport!

After a ten-minute stop at our five-star super-deluxe hotel, which was to prove a real oasis for me during my four-night stay in Tenerife, we were off on our first excursion. 'Come on, Jeremy! You can't afford to look sleepy, mate! We're off to one of the best nights out in Playa. It's called Mutiny on the Bounty, and the great thing is that the kids can drink as much booze as they like. It's all included in the price of the ticket,' Paul urged, as I tried desperately to hail a taxi to make a quick escape. I had a feeling that *I* might be joining a mutiny, but it wasn't likely to involve taking any of the now-exuberant teenagers with me.

The short coach trip to a large warehouse on the edge of town revealed just how much energy was needed to keep the holidaymakers going. Paul was definitely 'givin' it large': he made them all sing a song that had been at the top of the UK charts and goes something like this: 'We're lovin' it, lovin' it, lovin' it, we're lovin' it like this.' It soon became the most irritating tune I'd ever come across, simply because of the number of times I had to listen to it sung by the drunk and incapable.

I glanced at my watch as we arrived at this happening night-spot, and saw that it was already nine p.m. It soon became clear that this was a themed night of entertainment based, as you might expect, around a ship and its crew.

Rather interestingly, though, there was no sign of Mr Christian or, for that matter, Captain Bligh. Instead we were greeted by the Blue Pirate, and his adversary the Red Pirate. I began to feel as if I was back in panto playing Mr Smee alongside Captain Hook in *Peter Pan*. I was allocated to join the team of the Blue Pirate, and somehow, as I looked on at the four-hundred-plus party-goers, I had the feeling that it was going to be a long haul to one o'clock, when the party was due to finish.

After an hour of asking me if I was 'that bloke from *Airport*' and taking my picture for the folks back home, the Blue Pirate's team were tucking into chicken-in-a-basket meals. I'd already delivered enough beer and wine to them to put a small brewery out of business, and the assembled crowd showed no sign of wanting to stop drinking. The hordes were getting more inebriated by the minute, and there was nothing I could do to escape as the live entertainment started. The very first things to come on stage as the drunk audience yelled, 'We're lovin' it, lovin' it, lovin' it,' were two Ukrainian dancers clutching huge great pythons! Things couldn't get any worse for me than this: not only could I not have a drink – I was on duty, you know – I was being confronted by snakes. A living nightmare!

'Jeremy, we need you to help us, please!' came a somewhat desperate plea from one of the reps over the din of revellers. 'What's up?' I yelled back.

'A girl over here is having trouble breathing and we need to get her outside!'

My immediate concern now was to help the girl. As we struggled with her friends to get her outside into the fresh air, Paul joined us and arranged for one of the Thomson's drivers to take her to the hospital, which was just round the corner. The girl, who had asthma, had been overcome by the revelry and drinking. Although it was rare for Paul to have to deal with people collapsing from chronic medical conditions, he often had drunk and disorderly clients who ended up in hospital or at the police station. 'Just last week I was in one of the clinics with someone who'd had one too many and had fallen off the bus,' he said, in his ever-exuberant way. By now he was busily ushering his group on to the buses for the next leg of our marathon night on the tiles.

I was left wondering what possessed a man like Paul to spend nigh on twenty hours a day chasing around looking after people and their excesses, and all for just £7000 or so per annum! Madness gone crazy!

'Can I not catch my breath, please, Paul?' By now I was begging him to let me go home early. 'Paul, do you *really* need me to come into this club with you? It's just after one a.m. and I'm completely knackered. My wonderfully comfy bed is screaming for me to rest my weary bones.'

The ever-ready rep responded emphatically, 'Jeremy, we've got another three or four hours of partying still to go. You can't be a lightweight now, you know. If you want to be a Freestyle rep, you need to put the hours in, mate! Let's party!'

I turned to Simon, the cameraman, and gave one of my Paddington Bear stares down the lens, which needed no explanation. Simon just laughed and said, 'Stick with it, mate. Only another two nights to go!'

Although Simon, as always, had the very best intentions, his statement wasn't too comforting. I had no idea how I was going to get through another two nights of 'givin' it large' as a young holidaymakers' rep. But Paul was dragging me off in the direction of a nightclub entrance before I could say any more to Simon. He soon learnt how tricky being recognized can be. Why?

Well, if you've ever been to Tenerife you'll appreciate that it is swarming with fellow Brits, most of whom watch television, 'Oh, look, it's that bloke from BBC One – what's his name,' shouted a girl from the West Country, who had just spotted me and my crew edging our way into the club.

'Oh, yeah! It's Jeremy – let's get a picture!' Twenty-five minutes, and about seventy photos later, Paul realized that the situation was becoming uncomfortable for me and the crew, as people were crushing us against a bar. 'Jeremy, you'd better get off before something unruly happens.' Finally, Paul had seen sense and was releasing me for a few hours' sleep. Before we could leave, though, Nicky the director needed us to film Paul letting me off the hook. Thankfully this simple task was over in just five minutes and I headed back to my five-star oasis.

The following morning, after just five hours' sleep, I was off to catch up with Paul at the Los Piramides hotel, where we would be giving a welcome briefing to all of the guests who had arrived in Playa the day before. 'Paul – morning, mate. This is hideous! It feels very early even though it's nine o'clock! How much sleep did you get?' This seemed like a logical question for me to ask, especially as I'd left him partying in the nightclub with the revellers from the Mutiny excursion.

'Oh, I got into bed at about five-thirty, so it was an early night for me,' he responded, in his effervescent manner.

'An early night? You're having a laugh, Paul!'

'I often don't get to bed at all,' he said. 'It's important that we stay with the guests if they want us to. It's our responsibility to make sure they have a truly memorable holiday.'

I'm sorry, but my sleep is far too important to me. I was already realizing that this wasn't a job for the weak and feeble: you needed the stamina of an ox to keep up with the never-ending pace.

Paul Mobbs was supervising a team of six Freestyle reps, charged with the unenviable task of entertaining the

30,000 or so young visitors who travel with the company to Tenerife every year. Their main responsibility was to sell the company's excursion programmes. You know the sort of thing – these are the extra trips that are not included in the price of your basic holiday, where you get a chance to go off and see the sights of your holiday spot. There was, however, as you might expect, one big difference with the excursions Lisa, Darren and Paul were trying to sell: none of them involved any sightseeing whatsoever. Each excursion was simply an opportunity to see how much beer and spirits the punters could consume. Believe me, some had already proved the night before that they had hollow legs! Lisa, who has been a rep in Tenerife for a number of years, like Paul, got up on to the stage to introduce herself to the forty-odd guests who had managed to get out of bed to join us. To be honest, they wouldn't have made it had we not woken them up. She immediately let rip, 'givin' it large', selling the company's boozy trips. Her performance made it crystal clear that you needed to have a never-ending source of energy to get yourself through each day. The briefing lasted almost an hour, during which time each of the reps stood shouting at the guests trying to get them into the holiday mood.

No, really, there's no need to ask! Naturally I declined the offer of a chance to jump around the stage like a semi-deranged baboon offering my wares, preferring instead to chat with some of the new arrivals about how they expected the reps to make their holiday brilliant. 'So, girls,' I began, 'what do you want from the reps while you're here?' One of six girls, who were all eighteen and awaiting their A-level results, said, 'That Darren's okay, he can do anything he wants to me.'

I wasn't at all surprised, especially not after some of the scenes I'd witnessed as I went around the hotel trying to wake people up. And before you ask, it was all a bit too graphic for me to go into any detail here. Suffice it to say, anyone over the age of consent, I'm sure, would have done the same, given half a chance.

'That's not really what I had in mind, girls. Do you think you'd like to do the job yourselves?'

After much deliberation another girl, who was now comfortable with the camera being pointed at her, replied, 'The thing is, it's down to the reps to make your holiday go with a swing. Most of us have never been away from home without our parents before, so we just want them to make sure we can party and enjoy ourselves. I don't think any of us here would want the job, but they choose to be reps so it can't be all that bad, can it?' The girls were all nodding sagely in agreement. So there you have it: they don't want the job but they expect those that do it to be all-singing, all-dancing all the time.

Dictionaries and encyclopedias define a 'holiday' as a day set apart for religious observance, or for the commemoration of some extraordinary event or distinguished person, or some other public occasion. Needless to say, the word 'holiday', for most of us, now means those two all-important weeks in the sun where we can fight every day to get a golden tan to make colleagues and neighbours jealous. However, for some of the young revellers I was having to wet-nurse it was clear that a tan was the last thing on their minds.

The traditional 'wine, women and song' was certainly the order of the day for a bunch of guys I found looking very much the worse for wear near the bar. I took a deep breath so that I wouldn't be bowled over by the alcohol fumes emanating from them and asked, in a tone reminiscent of a cannon going off, 'So, do you think this holiday would be as good if it wasn't for Paul and the other reps?'

As one took some aspirin he replied, in a broad Scottish accent, 'No way. The reps, especially that Paul, are quality!' Sadly, that's about all I could get from the group, who just wanted to crawl off to rest before another packed night on the town.

Paul and I spent the next couple of hours patrolling the pool area of the hotel, checking that the semi-conscious holidaymakers were all OK. 'None of them are very brown, are they, Paul?'

He grinned. 'No, most of them come out here two days before they're due to go home and fry for as long as they can. At least that way they'll have some colour about them.'

He was right: as I wandered around the edge of the pool, most of the hung-over youngsters were frantically trying to tan in ultra-fast time. It's sad, really: most of them spend their time trying to get drunk or take people to bed without really relaxing, which is what I thought a holiday was all about.

Sorry – I'm beginning to sound like an old git, I know! I can hear you ask, 'Were you ever young, Jeremy? Did you ever party?'

Yes, of course, and I've had one too many like most of us. In fact, I can remember being with some close Russian friends on holiday once when it was decided we would have a few beers. The beers soon turned into vodkas, and ten or so litres later we were all doing very foolish things that attracted the attention of the local police. I'm not going into any real details here: all you need to know is that none of us could find our clothes when asked where they were by the less-than-amused bobbies!

It was approaching one p.m., and I was already feeling the effects of not getting to bed earlier the night before when I discovered that I was needed to join Paul and his colleagues on a catamaran. Now, the catamaran takes those who have the energy, and aren't feeling too sick, out into the Atlantic

Ocean to photograph the dolphins who like to swim along-side it. 'This is an important trip, Jeremy. It's really the only chance the kids get to do anything really tourist-like.'

'Are they going to be okay, this lot, on a boat?' I had to ask. 'Isn't it all going to seem a bit sedate in comparison to the other excursions they do?'

Once again Paul was laughing at my less-than-enthusiastic face. 'No worries, the boat's got loads of booze on board so they'll all be able to catch the hair of the dog.'

Great! There was I thinking I was going to have a nice quiet sail around the harbour, looking at the wildlife and relaxing for the first time since I'd arrived in Tenerife, and Paul was expecting me to help him man a bar and enable the assembled hordes to get sloshed again! HELP!

If I had had to blame one man for my current predicament, I guess it would have to have been the late Mr Thomas Cook. Yes, I do mean the man who started one of Britain's best known travel agencies! Dear Mr Cook, a former Baptist preacher from Market Harborough, was struck by the idea, while walking to Leicester to attend a temperance meeting, 'of employing the great powers of railways and locomotion for the furtherance of social reform'. He chartered a train to travel with his temperance group the overwhelming distance of just twelve miles between Leicester and Loughborough to join colleagues. The return journey cost each of the delegates a shilling, and proved an outstanding success. Cook later commented, 'Thus was struck the keynote of my excursions, and the social idea grew upon me.' The very first profit-making trip for Cook personally took place in 1845 when he ran an excursion to Liverpool.

Today not only does his name live on in the form of the travel agency and holiday companies, but that of his son also, John Mason Cook, who joined his father's business in 1864. Two years later he organized the first tour to America.

The bright green image of JMC Holidays – John Mason Cook – is now familiar to many of us. If only Thomas knew then what he was unleashing on the world and, more specifically, upon your humble author! In Tenerife I was beginning to regret not being able to time travel like Doctor Who: I was eager to chat with Mr Cook and put him straight about all of this package-holiday palaver, although I'm not sure he'd find me too temperate, given the problems I was encountering as a holiday rep. To be honest, poor Thomas Cook would probably have had a seizure if he'd had to witness the boozy mayhem and semi-debauched nature of the modern Young Persons' Holiday!

Many of our guests were feeling green around the gills, apparently, as they sat, subdued, on the deck of the catamaran. Paul was desperately trying to liven them up and get them back into the party spirit, but most were concentrating hard on not being sick, and didn't even want to see the sandwiches I was thrusting under their noses. Well, let's face it, I need to get my own back sometimes!

'Paul, why do you bother with this job? It's never-ending, and they don't seem to appreciate the effort you put in on their behalf, do they?' was the perfect question to ask while everyone else was quiet.

Paul, who had joined the British Army when he first left school, then left to join his local Fire Brigade, replied, 'I'd always done things to please my parents, especially my dad, but I'd fancied working overseas too, so when the chance came up to work as a holiday rep it appealed to me. I can't see myself doing anything else for a long while yet. I love every minute. It may seem like this lot are ungrateful at the moment, but when you look at the comments book when they leave, they all say how much they've enjoyed holidaying with me and my team.' That was it! Everything I needed to know was in Paul's last few words: 'They've enjoyed holidaying with me and my team.' Paul was doing this because he wanted to be on a perpetual holiday.

Lisa, his sidekick, was less enthusiastic about life as a rep: 'I've had enough of the job, to be frank. The hours are long, you only get one day off a week, and you're on the go for ten months of the year like this. I miss my folks back home, and just crave being able to curl up in front of the telly with a box of chocs watching a soppy film.'

Finally, I'd met someone who was talking sense about this job. 'How do the others view being a rep?' I asked her.

'Darren and the others are only nineteen themselves, so they're out here earning a bit of cash, having fun and partying. None of them views this as a long-term career. It's just a way to keep the tan going and have a few beers.'

We followed the dolphins for an hour, and the crowd perked up when we dropped anchor in a small bay to swim. Then we entertained them on the boat with drinking competitions. Now, there's a surprise!!

As you know, we often need to film something from several different angles to edit a film together. The catamaran was no exception to this rule and we needed to take some shots of the boat from another craft. As luck would have it, Nicky, our director, had arranged for a speedboat to pull up alongside so that Simon and the sound recordist, Guy, could get some shots of us all partying like mad in the warm Atlantic waters. Always on the lookout for ways to escape the incessant drinking, I saw my chance and hijacked the speedboat so that I could scurry back with my crew to harbour. As I waved goodbye to everyone, Paul shouted, 'You need to be at the Los Piramides by eight – we've got the popcorn party tonight, mate, and that's the mother of all nights.'

Wonderful! If there had been a Great White Shark in the vicinity, I'd probably have thrown myself into the Atlantic and taken my chances – anything to put myself out of my misery.

Now, if you're curious about what a popcorn party is, I can assure you that I was too. I didn't have long to wait to find out. After just an hour's rest back in Quietville, the nickname I'd given my hotel, I found myself ushering people on to yet another bus. The mood on the coach was electric as Lisa played a variety of group games with the young party animals. She'd already explained to everyone that 'You can drink as much as you like, fill your boots, it's all included in the price of your tickets!' The thought of them all filling their boots, as she put it, was enough to tip me over the edge. I was now feeling about ninety-five, and craving a quiet little taverna somewhere where I could sample the local food, hear myself think, and enjoy some stimulating conversation without the fear of someone chucking their guts up over me.

As we approached the venue for the party I asked Nicky, 'Do you mind if I don't come into this place just yet? Can I wait until we get to the popcorn part of the evening? I'm all larged out, I have to say.'

Nicky, who herself had grown tired of trying to film with people shouting, 'Hello, Mum!' at the camera, relented. 'It's probably safer if you stay here anyway, Jeremy. Simon, Guy and I will get the generic shots we need for the film, and when the popcorn thing starts we'll let you know.'

I should explain to you now that the idea behind this popcorn party is for everyone to get paralytic before the organizers fire tons and tons of popcorn across the top of them while they're dancing to all manner of songs including, of course, 'Lovin' It, Lovin' It, Lovin' It'. Then Paul and the other reps encourage everyone to try to push as much of the popcorn as possible into places you wouldn't imagine it could get.

At last the moment came, and I could put off joining the now-sloshed crowd no longer. I've never witnessed anything like it in my life. There were approximately nine hundred seventeen- to twenty-two-year-olds all thrusting huge quantities of popcorn down each other's clothing. The noise was deafening, and the resident DJ was encouraging them all to be as cheeky as possible. Later a girl shook her trousers for me and, no word of a lie, a not inconsiderable hill appeared over the top of her boots, which were covered in vomit.

Afterwards, as Paul and I tried to herd them all on to the coaches for another nightclub crawl, people were being sick in every corner of the car park. Those that weren't being sick were busy trying to show the camera their backsides, which is oh-so-funny if you're drunk, but not when you simply want to go to bed. One lad from Manchester decided he wanted to shock Nicky by showing her his manhood. The following day I had great fun telling him that we'd been transmitting live to the UK, and that his mum had probably witnessed him waving it around while she was drinking her hot chocolate. In the end we confessed it was a wind-up, but not before he'd sweated for a few hours.

Did I end up 'lovin' it, lovin' it, lovin' it'? Certainly not! I can't say that I was sorry to be leaving the job behind as I checked in at the airport and said my farewells to Paul. Every holiday rep has to put up with an awful lot from the public, and I know from experience just how tough *that* can be. But people like Paul, who are charged with making the younger travellers' holidays fun-packed, really do win my admiration. The job requires you to be in the party mood for twenty hours a day, six days a week! The money is poor. OK, accommodation is provided and reps don't need to spend much money on food, but these are not rewards enough for me to give it all up and go to Tenerife – or what proved for me to be Tenegrife – as a rep.

# chapter seven
# JOURNEYMAN BOXER

**Salary:** £1500–2,000 per fight

**Requirements:** Applicants should have professional accreditation, be fit and willing to travel throughout the country to fights – and, above all, should not be frightened of seeing their own blood!

**Toughness rating: 10**

One look at yours truly tells you that I'm not necessarily the sporting type. In fact, the closest I get to physical exhaustion is when I have to pick up the TV remote control from the floor to change channels! So, you can imagine just how stressed I was to receive a briefing document on Shane Woollas, who is known as a 'journeyman boxer'. Given that I am supposed to be as deeply involved with each job as possible, my heart began to pound. I didn't mind the 'journeyman' part of the job, having spent most of my working life involved with travel, but I did object to this 'boxer' thing. With considerable reluctance, I packed my five-year-old

'Don't let the boss catch you with that cuppa, Jeremy. Slouching is forbidden!' Maggie & I catch a quiet moment to discuss the finer points of working for the Roger Barton Fish Empire.

Roger informed me that he didn't like slackers and that few new recruits lasted more than one shift working with him at Billingsgate market.

'Blimey mate, you certainly know how to live dangerously.
If Roger catches you mauling the fish you'll be turned into a fishcake!'

'Put that bleedin' salmon down Jeremy, and get back to work!'

Circus performers Julie and Tex stand with me in front of the Big Top, ready to lynch me if the show doesn't go well.

'This blade is real! No one said anything about Tex chucking
these in my direction … help! Can you hear me Mother?'

Caught in the act, Tex hurls his extremely sharp
blades at me in front of the audience.

Having just arrived in the village of Bethlehem to film with a shepherd,
I was eager to prove I'd been to this holy-sounding place.

My favourite farmers Nick and Kyra look on with some bemusement
at the thought of how busy I'm really going to be.

Kyra feeds my adopted lamb Tarzan who even now demands the very best food in the house. A sheep after my own heart!

As I stand with Dave 'Spiderman' Hulme at the top of Blackpool Tower, we discuss the pros and cons of 60-watt bulbs.

Dave and I dangle off the tower with nothing but dental floss-like rope to keep us there!

(Above) You said I was going to be starring in the remake of *Lawrence of Arabia*, not digging latrines!'

(Left and below) The men of the 187 squadron of 23 Pioneer Regiment in Oman relented and let me loose on a lorry and JCB digger.

Stately home owner Suzie was totally committed
to making Leighton Hall in Lancashire a success.

The 'hammer number five' team at the Morgan Platts industrial forge.

'If I pretend to be asleep, they might leave me alone?'
Catching forty winks between shifts loading iron bars into the furnace.

trainers – I'd only worn them once before – and headed, as instructed, for the Grimsby area.

I wasn't exactly filled with confidence as I approached Shane's home. I'd conjured up images of a successful boxer with a large mansion and a Ferrari in the drive. How wrong could I be! Shane was living with his wife and two small children in a run-down mobile home. Sense should have told me that if he was featuring in my series he was probably struggling in some way, and for a good reason that, no doubt, I would discover in time.

'Hi, you must be Shane,' I yelped, as the door to the caravan swung hard in my direction and almost knocked me out. 'Steady, boy, we're not in the ring now, you know.'

Shane was a BIG fella, who seemed a bit overweight and therefore relatively unfit to be a boxer. In fact, he made me look almost slim – OK, maybe I'm stretching the truth by several miles but I *felt* a tad thinner than normal! (Quite who I'm trying to kid here, I have no idea!)

'Ha, great, you're here, Jeremy. We can get straight on with the training,' Shane said. Marvellous! It was seven forty-five a.m., I'd had no breakfast and now I was having to go training. This was already beginning to feel like malicious torture, so I had to ask, 'Shane, why do you do all this?'

'Well, I enjoy boxing, and it's a great way to earn a few quid,' he replied.

This, however, wasn't explanation enough for me, and I hoped I would discover more about the reasons behind Shane's chosen career path.

Having managed to find a completely uninhabited stretch of quiet Lincolnshire road, which was a huge relief – I didn't want tons of people to see me have a respiratory attack – Shane and I began to jog at a steady pace. And before you ask, the pace was steady so that I could interview this big boxer while Simon the cameraman dangled himself out of the back of the BBC production car, driven by Natalie, my trusty researcher.

Things went well until a team from the Environment Agency decided to start work on one of the ditches adjacent to where we were attempting the interview. The noise of their strimmer was so loud that Guy, the sound engineer, was struggling to cope. If the sound is no good, we have to keep trying until we get it as near to perfect as possible. This is all well and good when you're sitting in TV studio armchairs, not having to exert yourself, but when the director, who in this case was Mike, wants you to keep jogging backwards and forwards for an hour, it's a damn nightmare, unless you've been training with the Kenyan National Marathon Team, which I had not!

By the end of the interview I was feeling rather proud of myself. Shane was looking decidedly more puffed out than I was, although to be fair he had been doing most of the talking. He'd explained to me, 'I've been involved with amateur boxing ever since I was a nipper. It was the best way to stay out of trouble in this area, and I always managed to keep in shape, although admittedly now I'm not as trim as I used to be. My dad always used to tell us to work at boxing, because if we were good at it we'd never have too many debts. Turning professional has been great, because now I can regularly earn two thousand pounds plus per fight.'

'It seems like a drastic way to earn a few quid, Shane,' I observed.

'It can be a bit bloody in the ring at times, but once the twelve minutes or so is over, I walk away with enough money to buy some more bricks for my house, which pleases the missus no end.'

Right! The mist that had fogged my understanding of why Shane would want to subject himself to physical abuse from another human being began to lift. Shane, it transpired, ran his own business laying driveways and patios and had purchased a plot of land on which to build his wife's dream home, which was why he and the family were living in the caravan. His sideline as a journeyman boxer – which, according to the director's notes, was a professional boxer prepared to travel anywhere in the country at the drop of a hat to fight any and all comers, to include world-class boxers wishing to train – was proving an excellent way to supplement his income, thus enabling him to finish his house sooner than he would otherwise have expected. But I still wasn't convinced that being a professional boxer was the best way for anyone to try to raise a few bob – think of the pain! – and certainly had a few more questions for Shane about why he was pursuing such a path.

On our way back to Shane's home, I began to read some notes Natalie had given me from the British Boxing Board of Control (BBBC). The Board has had responsibility for overseeing professional boxing in Britain since 1929, and issuing licences to people like Shane. Approximately two thousand professional fighters are registered with the BBBC, of which 650 are active boxers, our man being one of them. One of the documents included in my pack was entitled 'Career as a Professional Boxer', and this I had to read. It states, 'Professional boxing is a hard, demanding sport and, like so many other areas of activity or sport in which young men like to participate, there is a degree of risk.' *Risk!* No, thanks, folks, no risk for me. Fortunately, I'd clarified with Mike just how much involvement I was going to have in this film: 'Don't be silly, Jeremy, we don't want you getting in the ring to fight, we merely expect you to help Shane train and then be present at one of his professional bouts.' Phew! Not that I was about to offer myself up as a human punch-bag anyway.

As we pulled on to Shane's plot of land, an older chap of average build was waiting for us. 'Who's that, then, Shane?'

'Oh, he's trouble. That's my dad.' Shane smiled. 'He acts as my manager and trainer for the boxing.'

'Jeremy, nice to meet you. How did this morning's training session go?' asked Dave Woollas, Shane's dad, who looked like he'd fought in the ring himself a few times.

'Marvellous, thanks, Dave. But I need to sit down and have a bit of a rest, mate, I'm afraid.' As I started to chat with Dave about his involvement in Shane's boxing career, Shane's wife handed the fighter an enormous fried breakfast. Unable to resist the temptation, I asked, 'Dave, should he really be eating that stuff if he's trying to get in shape?'

Mr Woollas senior, while not too impressed with his son's fitness level, chipped in with 'A hearty plate of grub is good for his energy levels. You have to take into consideration the fact that he's laying driveways and patios all day, which is pretty tough physical labour. A man needs plenty of energy, and a fry-up will do him no real harm.'

This was lost on me, I'm afraid: Shane weighed in at about nineteen stone and, in his own words, was unfit. It struck me that huge plates of fried food were perhaps not the sort of thing a coach should encourage his charge to eat!

A brief chat off-camera with Shane's wife revealed that while she wasn't too keen on him fighting, she wanted the house built, so needs must. I was getting more concerned for the big fella by the minute. Did he enjoy boxing? I guessed I needed to stick with him to find out.

Now, as a man who has no knowledge of boxing whatsoever, I was desperately trying to learn a thing or two about the sport, which can be traced back all the way to ancient Greece, where it had featured in the very first Olympic Games. 'Shane's a heavyweight boxer,' Dave informed me, which seemed obvious, given his size, not that I knew what this meant in terms of boxing. Apparently there are seventeen recognized weight categories in boxing, although most professional boxers only fall into about eight: flyweight (up to 112lb/50.7kg); bantamweight (118lb/53.5kg); featherweight (126lb/57.1kg); lightweight (135lb/61.2kg); welterweight (147lb/66.6kg); middleweight (160lb/72.6kg); light heavyweight (175lb/79.4kg); and finally heavyweight, where the boxer can weigh anything from 195lb/88.5kg upwards. Sorry, I know that this information may be too much for most of you, but as I learnt it I thought you should too.

Chatting with Dave was humorous, to say the least. It struck me that he was a bit of a wide-boy, in the nicest sense. Dave explained that often he gets information about an opponent boxer that he doesn't share with his son. 'Is this true, Shane?' I asked, noting that Shane had finished his gut-busting fry-up in just a few minutes.

'Yeah, there was one fight with a Russian that I'll remember as long as I live,' exclaimed Shane. He went on to describe how he'd entered the ring, 'giving it large' to his signature tune – which all good boxers have, I'm told – when the lights went out and a spotlight shone across the wall towards the dressing-room entrance. There, emerging into the light, was an enormous Russian boxer, who was as wide across the shoulders as Shane was around his girth. Shane described him as looking something like 'a herd of buffalo stuck together. He was bloody huge.' Needless to say, the mighty Russian bear flattened Shane, who managed to go the distance but looked much the worse for wear. Dave, I discovered, rarely told his son specific details about a fighter, preferring instead to say, 'You'll easily beat him. This is the one that'll make you a star!'

Before Shane and I could head with Dave to the gym in Grimsby to continue our training, which I wasn't necessarily looking forward to, we had to finish preparing a driveway that Shane had started working on the day before. The sun had finally decided to grace us with its presence and the temperature had risen, leaving us both grafting like mad in the midday heat – not to be recommended, I can assure you. I could scarcely believe the situation: if Shane worked this hard all day, where exactly was he supposed to find the energy to box in the evenings? 'You just do! Once I'm in the ring the adrenaline starts to pump and I'm there focused on trying to win,' was his explanation. This guy clearly enjoyed boxing, although for the life of me I couldn't imagine why.

A coffee break gave me a chance to chat with Shane's customer about the progress of her drive. 'Well, what do you think of our efforts, then?' I asked, expecting the middle-aged lady called Helen to lavish praise on us for all the hard work we'd done.

'It's not bad, but you're a bit behind schedule,' came her somewhat caustic reply. Needless to say, I felt slightly upset, having literally worked myself into the ground.

Helen, though, had known Shane for a few years so she was the ideal person for me to ask, 'What do you think of his boxing exploits, then?'

She stood and thought long and hard. 'Well, he's never broken his nose, which is something, I guess. Personally I cannot understand why anyone would want to put themselves through all that, but I know he's desperately trying to build his own home without borrowing money, so I suppose he's not got much choice. I wouldn't want to have to pick up the pieces after each fight, though.' While she didn't necessarily appreciate how hard we'd worked on her drive, she had a complete understanding of Shane's situation.

Dave, who does a bit of building himself, arrived at around four o'clock to take us both to Grimsby. He'd spent the day preparing for a couple of funerals (oh, sorry, I forgot to mention he's also a funeral director!). 'Come on, boys,' he said, 'time to hit the road. It's going to take us about forty minutes to get to the gym.' He pushed us towards the car as we dragged our training kit behind us.

Grimsby, once one of Britain's busiest fishing ports, has been reduced to almost nothing. The heady days of the 1950s, when you couldn't move on the quayside for vessels unloading fish, have long gone. I was therefore surprised to find a thriving gym in the docks, absolutely heaving with young lads, all training frantically in the hope that they might one day follow Shane and move from amateur boxing to the professional circuit.

As soon as we got inside, a man thrust a skipping-rope into my hands. Dave introduced him to me: 'Jeremy, meet Joe, he's a professional boxing promoter.' Joe Frater, a Jamaican, had arrived in Grimsby thirty-odd years earlier with not a penny to his name. He now ran a successful boxing promotion business as well as a garage.

As a young man, he had been Jamaica's boxing official on the world circuit, so as I skipped and tripped for Britain I thought he was the ideal person to talk to about Shane. 'I've known Shane now for a number of years, and he's always been a keen boxer. The thing to remember is that many boys need an outlet for their energy, and boxing is a great way of constructively venting excess energy,' he explained. While Joe had always been a keen fan of boxing – his office was bedecked with pictures of him with some of the world's greats, like Lloyd Honeygan, Prince Naseem Hamed, Henry Cooper and, of course, Cassius Clay . . . oops, that was his original name, I mean Muhammad Ali – he'd never fought in the ring himself. He had clearly sussed that promoting was not only lucrative but also much safer than the sport itself.

Joe looked on with Dave as Shane embarrassed me with his skipping-rope tricks – although, it has to be said, the director and crew were amazed that I could even skip! Admittedly there'd been a number of calls to the police from concerned locals wondering if Grimsby was experiencing an earthquake!

'Jeremy, come on, I need you to help me hold this punch-bag for Shane. He needs all the practice he can get.' Dave threw one of those heavy great punch-bags in my direction – nearly winding me as I caught it. 'Keep those arms up, Shane! Come on, hit the damn thing like you mean it!' Dave was now being really ferocious with his son. Why was he so keen to push the lad towards an early grave? He explained to me, 'I've always encouraged Shane to do what he wants. He's always been mad on boxing and, rather than leave him in the hands of someone who doesn't care, I'd rather give him all my support.'

I picked myself up off the floor – I hadn't been watching properly while Shane was punching the bag. 'What's the story, then, Shane?' I asked, trying to catch my breath.

Shane had a thoughtful expression on his face as he replied, 'As I said earlier, I've been boxing since I was young. Dad always encouraged me to have a go, and I guess I do it for him as much as for the money. I know I'm probably never going to be a big name in the sport, but you have to chase the dream, don't you? Boxing enables me to earn enough money to build the wife and kids a home and that's the priority right now.'

Dave interrupted. 'Shane, enough chit-chat, you need to work a bit harder if you're going to be in shape for your next fight.'

I thought this was the right moment to leave them to argue the toss about the pros and cons of working with family members. It had been agreed that I would meet them again, with Joe Frater, ten days later in Sheffield, where Shane had a bout arranged.

Having battled my way on a Friday night along the M1 to reach Sheffield, I found Shane in one of the stadium's dressing rooms being examined by the BBBC doctor. Since 1950, when the BBBC set up its Medical Committee, it has closely regulated and monitored the well-being of its licensed boxers. In fact, the policing of its medical rules has become one of the Board's primary activities. I was hoping, however, that Shane wasn't going to be needing a doctor after the match . . . I had my fingers crossed!

Tension inside Shane's dressing room was running high, and all getting a bit too much for Natalie and me, so we decided to step outside for a few minutes' breather. What greeted us was a scene I shall never forget. Natalie and I were horrified. Shane's opponent was in the corridor practising his technique with his trainer. Why were we horrified? Well, it appeared that Dave, yet again, had managed to stitch up poor old Shane. His opponent, who weighed in at just under sixteen stone, was young, fit and very agile, with a washboard stomach. There was no doubt in my mind that this was going to be suicide.

'Shane, don't want to worry you, mate, but have you seen your opponent?' was the only thing I could ask when Natalie and myself returned to his dressing room.

'Oh, I've no doubt my dad's done it again,' was all he said.

There wasn't much I could say to that, so I just sat waiting for the awful moment to arrive when Mr Woollas junior would be doing battle in the ring with Mr Woollas senior standing by.

The moment of truth arrived. I picked up the all-important buckets of water and Shane's towel, and Shane and I headed for the ring with the camera crew hot on our tail. The crowd were jeering and shouting obscenities at Shane, who seemed oblivious to what was going on around him as he focused on the job in hand. According to Joe Frater, who had a ringside seat to watch Shane's performance, 'Shane's opponent, Jeremy, is a local lad, so the crowd will be behind him. Shane needs to keep the punches coming if he's to stand a chance of beating him. I've represented Shane for a number of fights and he's got what it takes! Honestly, you might not think so, but Shane was once a regional champion around these parts. He has always shown determination to win, and seems to enjoy the sport, even if he's not the fittest person on the circuit. To be honest, though, I'll be amazed if Shane wins this particular bout. Have you seen the opposition?'

For the first time since I'd embarked upon filming this story, I could see where someone involved in boxing was coming from: 'Joe, I know, mate, I'm very afraid for him,' was about all I could utter as the bell rang for the first of four three-minute rounds.

Shane was struggling from the off, as his opponent leapt all over the ring throwing punch after punch. In fact, the ratio of punches appeared to me to be something like eight to one in his opponent's favour. I'd never before watched a boxing match, and was not sad that I'd missed the opportunity to see grown men hitting each other. The one consolation, though, was that they were fighting under the Queensberry Rules, which had been developed in 1867 by a boxer named John Graham Chambers. Chambers had formulated his rules under the auspices of John Sholto Douglas, 9th Marquess of Queensberry. The Queensberry Rules were intended to fine-tune the existing boxing regulations to ensure a fighter's safety. For example, they incorporate a code that defines the grounds on which a bout can be stopped, ensuring that serious injury is not inflicted on contestants who have not been knocked out but are no longer able to defend themselves. The first regulatory standard in boxing had been drawn up in 1743 by John Broughton, who included one specific rule to prevent fighters hitting their opponents when they were down. This rule had been kept by Chambers, for which I was very grateful: if Shane was going to end up on the deck I wanted him to stay there and admit defeat, even though he had earlier declared, 'I never throw in the towel, I either get knocked out cold, or I fight to the end.' What was all this madness about? Good question!

As the minutes of the first round plodded on, under the watchful eye of the BBBC officials, who ensure the regulations are adhered to at all times, I tried once again to fathom Shane's reasons for boxing. He was a likeable guy, who always had something intelligent to say. He clearly enjoyed the challenge of boxing, and dreamt of being world class, but the only reason I could find for him to be in the ring was money, pure and simple. That house needed building and he needed the money to build it.

Thank God, the bell rang for the end of the first round. Shane was looking shattered as he sat down in the corner and his dad thrust a large bottle of water into his hand. Sadly for Shane, his father started to offer him advice about what he should be doing to win. Personally, I felt like telling Dave that perhaps the best advice he could give Shane would be 'Give in.' After all, I'd learnt from Joe that Shane was guaranteed to collect his fee, whether he lasted the four rounds or not. This was madness gone completely barking!

Round two was more of the same sorry scene as Shane struggled to keep going. And remember that, unlike his opponent who was being paid a salary by a professional promoter to dedicate his entire time to his boxing, Shane had been shifting eight tons of hard core by hand for somebody's patio earlier that day, and should have been tucked up in bed getting some rest. Because there was little chance that a promoter would employ him full time, he was unable to rely on his income from boxing and forced to work laying driveways. This is typical for most boxers and even the BBBC advises people of this in its literature: 'For most boxers their ring earnings will act as a boost to their ordinary earnings and all potential professionals are therefore advised to ensure that they have a good regular income, which they can maintain during their boxing career. A sympathetic and understanding employer is always an asset.' It was definitely a good job that Shane was his own boss.

By the time round four had started I was feeling exhausted just watching. It was clear that Shane, who was now bleeding all over the ring from several cuts to his face, was struggling to stay on his feet. The determination on his face, however, showed that he would stay true to his word and fight to the bitter end, no matter what that end might be. In fairness to Shane, he had landed a number of good heavy left hooks upon his opponent, who himself was flagging – Shane having the weight advantage over him.

When the bell rang for the end of the bout, the relief on my face was apparent to Simon, my cameraman, who had spent most of the fight running round trying to capture every essential moment, while being shouted at by the spectators to 'Get out of the bloody way!'

My parting comment to Shane was, 'Well, Shane, thanks for letting us film you, mate.' I then added mischievously, 'If I were you, I'd put your dad in the ring next time he wants you to take on someone like that, and see how long he lasted!'

Shane's response was only to be expected, really: 'Well, at least now I can afford to have those bricks delivered tomorrow.'

Having spent twelve agonizing minutes watching Shane punched about, I left him and Dave at the ringside with the same opinion I had had when I first met them. For me, boxing remains a pretty mad way of trying to make money. Shane, like so many other journeymen, is waiting for the moment when he is spotted for the big-time. Sadly, it happens to very few boxers. Perhaps the careers leaflet from the BBBC sums it all up in a nutshell: 'Professional boxing is not a career to be embarked upon lightly, but for the dedicated, determined and fit young man it may offer an area of opportunity in times where there may be very few others around.'

# chapter eight
# BLACKPOOL RIGGER

**Salary:** £15,000–18,000 per annum

**Requirements:** Applicants need to be fit, have a sense of humour, enjoy working in the great outdoors and have a good head for heights.

**Toughness rating:** 10

You would have thought that by now I'd have cottoned on to the fact that when the *Toughest Job* production office call me my fate has already been sealed. There I was, happily sitting in the beer garden of a country pub not far from Eastbourne, when Juliet, the series producer, called to ask, 'How are you with heights, Jeremy?'

As you know, I'm somewhat foolhardy, and in the blink of an eye I replied, 'Fine! No worries!'

On reflection, this was most definitely the wrong answer. Let me explain why.

My instructions were simple: head for Blackpool and seek

out Spiderman. That was it and, yes, I did say Spiderman! And having accepted the challenge I wasn't really in a position to change my mind. Like many of you, I, too, have seen that crime-fighting super-hero in the comics and, yes, I was aware of his exploits on the sides of buildings. Was I worried? There can be no doubt about it. FOR SURE!

As I checked into my overnight accommodation, I decided to find out just how famous this Spiderman chap really was. 'Do you know where I can find Spiderman?'

The girl at Reception laughed and said, 'Oh, you mean Dave Hulme! He'll most likely be at the Tower, Mr Spake.' Great! Now my heart was racing! The office, in true production style, had failed to mention that Spiderman would most likely be at Blackpool's most famous landmark: its TOWER.

Needless to say, my mind was working overtime throughout the night, and my nocturnal unrest was so horrific that to say my bed looked as if Armageddon had arrived in Blackpool would be no understatement. Come on, folks, wouldn't you have been worrying about what exactly you would be facing in the morrow?

Rather unsurprisingly, I decided to skip breakfast, bite the bullet, and get myself down the road to the nearest . . . ummmmmm . . . railway station! My plan was thwarted by a rather crafty Liverpudlian member of the production team called Alison. I had worked with her for three months and by now she was pre-empting my every move: she had rather cunningly booked a taxi to take me from the hotel along the world-famous promenade to the Tower. It would be fair to say that the half-mile journey was one of the longest I have ever had to undertake. What made it worse was that I could see the blessed Tower every which way I went. My immediate thought? There could be no escape. At this point I was trying to convince myself that the SAS (Special Air Service) motto, 'Who Dares Wins', was appropriate to me. Then

I reminded myself that I would never in a million years have made it into the SAS, so it was about as much use to me as a chocolate fireguard!

With one faltering step from the taxi, I found myself inside the ground floor of the Tower. As I stood waiting for my researcher to meet me in Reception, I had a chance to read some more of my notes concerning Blackpool's most famous tourist attraction. Did you know, for example, that construction of this rather imposing building began on 29 September 1891 and lasted two and a half years? Or that the Tower opened for the first time on Whitsunday, 14 May 1894? It cost £42,000 to build, and weighed in at a staggering 2586 tons, 2493 of which were made up of steel, with the remaining 93 being cast-iron. That's an awful lot of metal – in fact it's 518 feet 9 inches of metal, to be precise! I'd only been in the place about three minutes and was already regretting it.

'Sorry to trouble you, but, er, I'm . . . I'm, er, looking for the BBC team and Spiderman,' I asked, in broken tones. The woman at Reception was charming, and her soothing voice calmed me somewhat as she assured me, 'They're in the aquarium, which is just behind us here.' Phew! The ground floor, what a relief!

Alison greeted me, and asked me to follow her to the aquarium access area, where I could meet Dave. What confronted me was a stout fellow clad in diving gear. He looked like something from a James Bond film. 'If he was wearing diving gear, why do they call him Spiderman?' I hear you ask. That's exactly what was running through my mind. 'Why do they call you Spiderman, Dave?' was my first question after we'd been through the usual introductions.

'Well, Jeremy, I'm responsible for keeping the Giant Turtles' tank clean, so I need to get in there for a short while first, but once I'm out all will be revealed.'

As you know, the reason I'm sent to investigate Britain's weird and wonderful jobs is so that I can have a go myself, so I had to ask, 'Do you need me to join you in there, Dave?'

Thankfully, he informed me that my presence might make the turtles fractious, given that they had never seen me in their tank before. Don't they watch BBC Television? Once I'd caught sight of these majestic creatures I was rather sorry I hadn't been able to enjoy a swim with them, but I'm not sure what the public would have made of my large frame floating past the panoramic windows.

Dave had lulled me into a false sense of security and I was beginning to wonder what could possibly be tough about his job. Reality, however, was just around the corner. Dave emerged from his aquatic antics wearing a pair of overalls, and what looked like rock-climbing equipment. 'Ali-s-s-son, is that what I think it is? No, no, no, no. On second thoughts, don't answer that question. Ignorance is bliss, or so my mother assured me as a child.'

'Jeremy, don't worry, we've got some of that gear for you, boy!' was Alison's rapid retort. I didn't want to hear any more, especially as she was grinning from ear to ear, almost splitting her face in half.

Mike, the director on this, was already in film-making mode. 'Right, then, folks, let's get ourselves upstairs to the area we've picked for training.'

'Hello, sorry, training? Training for what?' I begged him to explain himself.

'Abseiling, of course!' he declared, with a semi-nervous grin.

'ABSEILING! You're having a laugh, you lot!' I can assure you that in fact the air was considerably bluer than I might have suggested here, and I continued to ramble almost incoherently about me and abseiling.

As I stepped out on to the works access point, which for

those of you who are interested is the bit on top of the roof of the brick structure at the bottom of the Tower, the insanity of Dave's job hit me. One glance straight up the 518 or so feet left all but the strongest among us feeling slightly nauseous. Dave ushered me towards a rather thin, middle-aged man, who was wearing a pot-holer's helmet. What was going on here?

Prompted by Alison, Mike introduced me to him. 'Jeremy, this is Chris. He's going to teach you to abseil, and as time is of the essence, we need to get straight on with it.' The urge to remind Mike politely about the madness of such a deed washed over me, but before I could argue with anybody, let alone Mike, Chris had harnessed me up, and thrust a small piece of string into my hands. 'Is this bit of string really going to be strong enough to hold my petite figure up there? And anyway, tell me about yourself, have you been abseiling long?' I was babbling uncontrollably in a desperate attempt to take my mind off what lay ahead. Chris was clearly a bit of a joker: 'I got the call from the Beeb yesterday, so rushed out to a camping shop and grabbed a book on rock-climbing.'

This really was not the time to be fooling around: I was about to lay my life on the line for the BBC, and they'd employed a complete half-wit to guide me to my demise. FABULOUS!

Chris encouraged me to grab my shunt, grapple with my lines, and get to grips with my karabiner, never mind remembering to lock off my stop and not mess around with a gri-gri. Does all this sound like complete nonsense? Try understanding it when you've got just *eight minutes* – no word of a lie – to learn it all before being sent over the edge. I can honestly say I have never been so focused or, for that matter, so sensible in my entire life. Dave watched as I was hooked up to the rope while still on *terra firma*, and Chris asked me to climb up a short but rather rusty ladder.

My ascent, while not long, had my heart pounding: I'd never dangled off anything from a piece of dental floss.

'Jeremy, you're going to have to let go up there. It's only about fifteen feet above ground and the rope really will be able to hold you. Remember what I told you about the shunt – bring it down with you,' Chris implored, in a firm but polite tone. A shunt, for those of you unfamiliar with such things, is an oblong-shaped piece of metal attached to a secondary rope. If for any reason your first rope fails or you start to descend uncontrollably, the shunt locks on the other line, preventing you falling to the ground – it's a safety device. At this point it was a good job that Chris was being polite, I can tell you. Launching myself off at the top of this short ladder, I came thundering to the ground. The rope had an awful lot of play in it considering it was supposed to be able to hold me easily.

It was at this point that I had to ask Dave what exactly we were going to do if I ever got to grips with the abseiling. 'Well, see up there, Jeremy?'

'Dave, I've looked once already, please don't remind me.'

'We're going to go up there, dangle off the top and change some of the ten thousand plus lightbulbs that are illumi-nated at night.' Eight years earlier Dave had clearly taken leave of his senses when he applied to work at the Tower. He had previously been employed on a chicken farm, which sounded a much safer environment to me. What on earth possessed a sane, intelligent human being to throw himself off the top of Blackpool Tower and change lightbulbs? Who knows? But I had a feeling I was about to find out.

'Jeremy, if you think that ladder was where the training ended and you can go home, you're very much mistaken. See that platform? Well, I want you and Dave to go up there and prepare to descend.' Chris was now being firm and direct with me, although he had paid me several compliments about the way in which I had quickly learnt what to do, most importantly to check everything ten times before I was satisfied it was going to be safe. The platform he had gestured towards was only about forty feet above the access area, and from below looked like a walk in the park. Who was I trying to kid?

'Is it not time for a tea break, Dave? Surely we deserve a tea break.' I was clutching at straws in the vain hope that Dave would let me off the job again. 'Sorry, mate, but we're behind schedule now and really do need to be getting on with the job.'

'Thanks,' was all I could muster by way of a response, as I was dragged screaming and kicking further up the staircase that every great tower contains in case the lifts break down.

I joined our cameraman, another Mike, who himself had been keen on abseiling for over twenty years, at the edge of this forty-foot drop, and suddenly felt very alone, even though Dave was there and would be descending with me. After five minutes spent trying to remember if my will was up to date, I took the bold step of popping myself over the railing and perching my knees on a ledge with my backside hanging in the wind. By now a gaggle of onlookers, all Tower employees, had gathered to watch the very first aircraftless major descent of Jeremy Spake.

Although I could hear Chris shouting instructions from below, it all went in one ear and out the other as I let go off the side. My knuckles had gone white from gripping so hard. Before I knew it, both Dave and I were back on *terra firma*, and I was smiling for the first time that day. 'Wow! What an experience! That was great fun – can I go home now?' Chris, who was clearly a professional at this abseiling game, said, 'You must be joking! Back up there! I need to see you and Dave abseil one more time and then we can go up to the top to get on with the job.' The second descent was even faster, and Dave had to work hard to keep up with me. After all, this was no longer new territory – I'd been up there before and survived!

Having successfully managed two descents in a row, I grabbed the opportunity to chat with some of the staff who had been watching. 'What do you lot make of Dave, then?' I asked.

'Mad,' was the unanimous response. One chap, who was painting, added, 'You wouldn't get me up there for all the tea in China! He and anyone joining him must be several dolly mixtures short of a pound.' It's funny, but a number of my friends were saying the same thing when I recalled my day at the Tower. Dave was clearly one of a unique breed of people willing to work on the edge of danger every day, and I had been foolishly led into his world in pursuit of the ultimate Tough Job.

It was no good, I couldn't put it off any longer. The time had come for me to ascend the Tower ready to start the major task of the day. We boarded one of the two lifts – which, by the way, clock up over fifty thousand trips a year between them – from the works access point to the observation deck, where we were greeted by a crowd of primary-school kids. The pressure was now on me: although I'd survived the abseil from forty feet, few people had been watching. Now I was not only going to have to contemplate abseiling with Dave some 480-odd feet above the promenade, but would also have the pleasure of a large audience to keep me on my toes.

For any of you who have been up Blackpool Tower, you will already know about the 'Walk of Faith'. For those of you who haven't, it is a piece of reinforced glass placed in the floor of the observation deck. People can walk across it looking straight down to earth! You cannot begin to imagine the diverse cross-section of human life that was struggling to pluck up the courage to walk across this glass. Having emerged from the lift with Dave, looking like something out of that Sylvester Stallone movie *Cliffhanger*, yours truly stood on the glass helping people find the courage to make the crossing.

'Jeremy, I'll be back in a minute.'

'OK, Dave, I'm happy here.' You're not kidding I was happy! All the time I stayed on the observation deck I was not having to dangle off the top of the Tower like some deranged fool on that piece of dental floss!

'Jer-Jere-Jeremy, come over here.'

I could barely hear Dave's muffled voice. Where was he? Suddenly, looking down through the glass, I caught a glimpse of him and Mike, the cameraman, standing on a thin, somewhat rustic-looking, scaffolding plank that ran parallel with the side of the Tower beneath me. 'Might I be so daft as to ask what the hell you two are doing out there, exposed to the elements, when it would be safer to stand inside like my good self?' Having been informed that Chris and Mike the director had also decided to leave their brains on the deck above and join them, I was instructed to get my bits and bobs in gear and get down there – 'The glass needs cleaning, Jeremy!' I was now on the verge of certifying Dave for referral to the nearest specialist hospital.

I passed through a hatch door – which is normally locked and should have stayed that way – down a short, somewhat precarious ladder and found myself exposed to the 20 m.p.h. winds, and a 430-or-so-foot drop.

By this point Dave had started to connect himself to the steel girders with his ropes and karabiner climbing clips – steel hooks that unscrew on one side, through which you pass rope, etc. He surely wasn't expecting me to hang out in the open beneath the observation deck of the Tower cleaning glass? 'No, you're all right, Jeremy, but I do need you to stay on the platform [plank would have been a better description], and pass me the mop and brush. This will help you get used to the height.'

'Dave, has it ever occurred to you that I might not want to get used to the idea of dangling up here in the wind?' Little did I know at the time that I was destined to spend nearly an hour on that thin piece of wood interviewing Dave about why he did the job.

I wasn't surprised to learn that he was the only person in Britain who could say that they worked as the official light-bulb rigger on Blackpool Tower. Surely no one else would be mad enough to want to venture down the outside of this Victorian structure, especially on their own. Admittedly, procedures were in place to keep track of Dave's movements but, nevertheless, it struck me as being one hell of a job, and I wasn't about to swap places with him.

But Dave was in his element: 'Jeremy, I'm my own boss up here, and have been since I started working with the ropes about eight years ago. Let's face it, management aren't really going to come out here looking for me. I simply couldn't be stuck in an office all day working nine to five, it would send me crazy.'

Sorry, I thought he was crazy already! 'There's plenty of danger in this job, isn't there? Is it this that appeals to you?' I asked, still trying to work out which one of us was madder than the other – Dave for doing it all the time or me for being daft enough to agree to join him.

'It's only dangerous if you don't think about what you're doing. You soon learn to check everything ten times up here,' replied Dave, with an unnerving air of confidence.

'What does your wife make of the life you lead, mate? Surely she worries about you?' I asked, as the wind whipped around the mighty landmark.

Dave promptly informed me that they had swapped jobs for a day for a short magazine article, and that his wife was well aware of what an average day was like for Dave Hulme. His experience of his wife's job serving people in a shop was a disaster as far as Dave was concerned: 'I don't know how the missus puts up with it.' Sadly, I never got the chance to meet her, so was unable to hear her thoughts on abseiling. Come to think of it, at this point I still didn't know what it would be like to abseil from such a height, having managed, more by luck than judgement, to avoid it.

While I continued to shout questions at Dave, who by now had started to abseil down the Tower replacing some of the larger bulbs, the film crew and director had repositioned themselves on the street below. Mike (the director – can you imagine how confusing it is when you have more than one Mike working with you?) was trying to encourage me, via a two-way radio, to lean right out over the girder so that Mike the cameraman could get a super shot of me and Dave chatting. How many of you watch television and think, Oh, isn't that a fantastic shot? I wonder how they did that. Well, let me explain: great shots on TV often mean great trouble for the poor presenter (I'm allowed to feel sorry for myself on occasions – no one else will), not to mention the poor person we have chosen to be our victim for a film, in this case my abseiling friend Mr Hulme. For twenty minutes the director had us shouting at the top of our voices at one another, while down below on the street everyone could hear us talking about life as the lightbulb man of Blackpool.

Finally, after freezing off parts of our anatomy, we were permitted to return to the observation deck, where Chris had cleared the area so that we could warm up. After I had dealt with the rabble of schoolkids that had crushed their teachers to get my autograph, I was informed that we needed to head straight up the locked ladders to about 480 feet and commence our descent on the outside of the Tower. I'd completely forgotten about the abseiling, because I had been as happy as Larry chatting with the kids and teachers.

I gathered up my karabiners, ropes, helmets, shunts *et al* and struggled up the narrow winding staircase with my heart in my mouth. I wasn't going to be able to put off the inevitable for much longer. I should explain that before I went up in the lift I had agreed with the director that he should lead by example, and join me over the edge of the Tower on a piece of string. As we climbed higher I caught Mike's eye, and he quickly engaged Alison in conversation about the wind, trying desperately to ignore my Paddington Bear stare.

During the couple of minutes it took us to climb to the point where Chris had been preparing everything for us, my life seemed to rush past my eyes. I stood thinking, I'm too young to die, I haven't been to Peru and seen Machu Picchu yet (sorry, one of my ambitions). Still, why worry? Dave does this five days a week, and is on emergency call in bad weather. Oh, yes, didn't I mention that Dave is out there in all weathers, and that only when the wind exceeds 40 m.p.h., and they have to turn off the lifts, does he stay inside to work? Wind, snow, ice and rain do not stop this incredible man from doing his job.

'Chris, why are my ropes connected to those shopping-bag handles up there?' I was now talking in a very irrational manner as I pointed at a couple of nylon straps.

'That's what we use. They're as strong as houses,' came his droll response.

'Sure, have you seen houses after a storm?' was my immediate retort, which cut no ice with this professional who'd heard every excuse in the book as I'd tried to get out of abseiling. I was instructed to carry out my own checks on the equipment to make sure I was happy with everything. 'Is this OK? Shouldn't that be there? Why is this here? I could have sworn it was there this morning.'

Ignoring me, Chris checked that Mike the cameraman was happy – I have to say Mike was a real brick, encouraging me and letting me know that it was OK to say when enough was enough. Once Mike had given the thumbs-up, Dave stepped over the railing to position himself ready to assist me. This was nothing but madness, the sun was shining and sensible people were lying on the beach getting a tan, which is where I should have been.

But it was no good: I'm one of those people who, if set a challenge, has to try to do it, no matter what. Dave was reassuring me that 480 feet really wasn't that far to fall, and that he had never had an accident, not even when he had to tether a large blow-up King Kong gorilla to the side of the Tower for one of its celebrations, or when he had to help paint the entire Tower gold for a centenary event. None of this was helping me, though, as I stood by the railing and suddenly realized why Dave had been nicknamed 'Spiderman' by his colleagues.

'There can be no doubt about it, your job is clearly tough, mate, I'm convinced. There's no need for me to continue, I'm off now, cheers.'

'Come on, it's great out here, and I really do need your help to get these bulbs changed,' was Dave's calm request.

Next thing I knew, without giving any thought to what I was really doing, I threw my leg over the railing, and joined Spiderman. What a feeling to be suspended 480 feet above the ground with nothing to hang on to except a thin piece of rope, and a couple of metal clips. The nerves I felt as I went over, which were obvious from the expression on my face, soon disappeared as Dave, who can only be described as a star, eased alongside me so that we could lower ourselves towards the area where the bulbs urgently needed replacing. The best thing you can do in such a situation, I discovered, is to put all your trust in the person you are with, and Dave had been abseiling up and down the Tower for seven years, and had had the advantage of doing an eight-day course in rope-work, as opposed to my stunning eight minutes. Still, there I was, feeling more comfortable, and happy to look at the wonders below me.

After about twenty minutes, during which we chatted about the charity work Dave does, and his involvement with St John's Ambulance, we set to work. It's trickier than you might expect, never mind that you are suspended way above the promenade. What you have to remember is that those bulbs are out there, like Spiderman, in all weathers, and many of them had rusted and got stuck in their holders. They broke in my hand as I tried to extract them. Never fear – Dave was on hand with a useful home-made gadget: the handle off the top of a small garden tool, which when pushed on to the broken bulb allowed me to turn the little blighter, releasing it.

Twenty or so bulbs later I was getting into the job, and hadn't even realized I was engaged in conversation with members of the public who had come up the Tower for the glorious view of Lancashire, and were looking over the railings directly towards me as I dangled from on high. I was definitely beginning to feel Dave's confidence rubbing off on me – can you imagine hanging 480 feet above Blackpool chatting with the public, who all wanted to know why I was no longer appearing in *Airport*? Bless them all, not one of them bothered to ask what the hell I was doing on the wrong side of the wire with lightbulbs in my hand. Clearly the world had gone mad!

I spent over an hour changing lightbulbs, then Dave offered me a beer downstairs in the Tower's world-renowned ballroom (of *Come Dancing* and Angela Rippon fame), which is home to an amazing Wurlitzer organ that, the officials of Blackpool claim, delivers almost eighteen thousand tunes a season.

As I sipped my beer I had time to reflect on Dave and his job. Tough it most certainly was, and I could only just begin to imagine what it must be like in the rain and snow. This is not a job for the faint-hearted, or for those who find heights disturbing. Bravery and fearlessness are great attributes to possess, and Dave appeared to have both in an unassuming way. He was on his own all day, and there wasn't exactly a host of people in the queue to help him – or, for that matter, to take his place.

I was offered the opportunity to join Spiderman again to change the entire ten thousand bulbs ready for the grand switching on of the Blackpool illuminations. Funnily enough, though, my search for the person with the Toughest Job had to continue. Handy, that. There can, however, be no doubt, that Dave's is near the top of the list.

# chapter nine
# PIONEER ENABLER

**Salary:** On joining an 18-year-old earns £10,344, rising to £29,182 per annum for a Warrant Officer Class 1.

**Requirements:** A sense of camaraderie, as well as the ability to work under extreme pressure often in hostile environments. Applicants with a knowledge of bricklaying, carpentry and general building/maintenance will be welcomed. Finally, any applicant unwilling to leave family and loved ones for long periods need not apply.

**Toughness rating: 14**

Having spent almost all of my childhood surrounded by Her Majesty's Royal Naval Dockyards and ships, because my dad served in the Royal Navy for almost twenty-five years, I never fancied a career in the armed forces. In fact, I can vividly remember telling dad that if he thought he was going to frogmarch me to the nearest recruitment office to sign up at the age of sixteen, he would probably be in need of exploratory neurological surgery to find out what was wrong with his thought patterns. Why? Well, I spent my formative years being barked at in true military fashion, feeling as though I had already set sail on behalf of the realm, and was put off taking orders from others for the rest of my life. I've never been much good at taking orders, especially when someone shouts them at me. Often I want to question the validity of certain instructions, which is how I know I wasn't cut out for military life.

You can therefore imagine my horror at learning from Alison in the office that I was about to join the British Army in pursuit of the nation's Toughest Job: 'Alison, there really is no need, love! I'm convinced already. Let's just accept that they've got it tough and look for something else, perhaps slightly less arduous. I can't bear it when people shout benign orders at me!'

'Sorry, Jezza, Juliet says that this is a must for the series and, anyway, it's already been arranged for you to report for duty early tomorrow morning at RAF Lyneham.' As visions of me bashing enough spuds for ten thousand hungry troops filled my head, I began to wonder why I had to go to an RAF airbase and not somewhere like Aldershot or Colchester, where the Army has a large presence. So I asked. 'Why do I need to report to the RAF, Alison? Surely I need to go to a garrison?'

'You will be, but first we all need to hitch a lift from the RAF as far as Thumrait airbase, where we will transfer to Camp South.'

Intrigued? I certainly was. I had no idea where on earth Thumrait or Camp South was, let alone what I would be doing once I got there.

Alison continued, 'I'll fax you a list of equipment you'll need, Jezza, and it's going to be great fun. I'm really looking forward to this film.' Like everyone else on the team, Alison could afford to be excited about the trip: not only did she know what was in store, but she could rest safe in the knowledge that she wasn't going to have to do any of the hard work that was inevitably involved in being a soldier. That, as always, was down to me, the poor uninformed presenter . . . and, yes, this is where you're supposed to feel sorry for me again. Never mind it being tough at the top, or so they say!

Fear is a terrible thing, you know, and I spent what seemed like an eternity sitting by the fax machine in my office waiting for the list to arrive, which I hoped would also tell me more about the job. My mind, as always, was running riot: I now had images of me lying on a stretcher in the back of a Land Rover ambulance, having collapsed from exhaustion on a twenty-mile yomp across open ground with one of those enormous backpacks strapped to my less-than-fit body! Shocking!

The buzz of the fax machine sent shudders down my spine, as the evil truth about my next task began to chug its way through. After the usual salutations from the production office, the fax went straight into a shopping list, failing, rather deliberately, to reveal any further information about my destiny at the hands of the Army. The list went something like this:

Sleeping bag
Knife and fork
Cup or mug
Water-bottle/canister
Sturdy boots
Long shirts
Long trousers
etc., etc., etc.

This all seemed pretty straightforward, and nothing much to worry about. That is, until I caught sight of the last three items:

Mosquito repellent
Anti-malaria tablets
Shamagh

Now, the mist was beginning to clear. Mosquito repellent and anti-malaria tablets meant I was heading for some tropical outpost. Thoughts of Belize in Central America sprang to mind, especially as the Army has been using this small country for tropical-warfare training for a number of years. However, the very last item on the list – a shamagh – meant Belize couldn't possibly be my destination. Why? Well, that's simple! They only wear shamaghs in one part of the world. Picture the Palestinian leader Yasser Arafat in his ubiquitous black-and-white headdress – it's a shamagh, and is worn by many men throughout the Middle East, and if I needed one in my luggage, I was most definitely heading for this arid part of the globe.

With true military precision my driver, Dave, delivered me into the clutches of the RAF at the allotted time of 0500 – or five a.m. to those of you who are not au fait with the military way of things. It was a gloomy and rather cloudy morning as I checked in with my film crew for the first leg of our twenty-seven-hour journey to Thumrait, which I had learnt from the briefing notes handed to me by Mike, the director, was situated at the southern tip of the Sultanate of Oman. I was right: the Middle East was to be my home for the next four days. What was the job? Pioneer enabler! Once again I was left feeling somewhat lacking in the information stakes. All I did know was that when I eventually arrived in Oman I was looking for Corporal Jim Reeves, who was a section commander in 187 Squadron of 23 Pioneer Regiment.

All this talk of the Pioneer Regiment meant little to me so, as my team and I boarded the C130 Hercules transport aircraft, I asked Mike, 'Do you know anything more about this "enabling" business?' Mike, who had already directed a vast number of the films in the series, had realized it was best to brief me as much as possible about the film, so he said, 'The Pioneers were described to me as the "Builders of the Battlefield". I hope this helps, Jeremy. Perhaps you'd like to read some of the background notes I was given on the Regiment.' Great! Not only was I having to join the Army, I was also going to be building!

Mike handed me an envelope and I tried to make myself comfortable for the seven-and-a-half-hour flight to Cyprus, where we would spend the night before continuing on to Oman, which would take a further seven hours to reach.

Now, anyone who has travelled in a C130 Hercules will be aware that this plane was not designed for great speed – nor, for that matter, comfort. In fact, it is positively bereft of anything half normal, and most certainly lacks the all-important first-class cabin that a discerning traveller such as my good self likes to see. I was shocked to see the service personnel from both the Army and Air Force scurrying round the aircraft after take-off looking for the best place to try to get comfy. Which, on the face of it, didn't seem possible, especially not with large pallets of freight filling the cabin. It was clear that some of the soldiers from the Royal Logistic Corps, who were travelling with us, had done this executive-style flying with the RAF before: they slung their hammocks over the aircraft's main structural spars and promptly went to sleep. If only I'd known, I'd have packed an inflatable mattress!

During the long and somewhat painful flight to Cyprus, I discovered from my notes that the British Government had authorized the largest deployment to Oman of our military personnel since the Gulf War. As I read on, it soon became apparent that the Pioneer troops were preparing to receive more than 22,000 personnel, who were due to take part in a joint exercise with the Omani forces. What all this meant for me was still not very clear.

The second leg of the journey to Thumrait had me convinced that being a soldier was about being as uncomfortable as it was possible to be. Cramped in the aircraft, I couldn't help but wonder what it would be like to be taken into battle carrying all my equipment in one of these planes. I can't imagine being in any fit state to do battle with the enemy after disembarking from a Hercules. But, then again, I'm not known for my shapely physique or soldiering qualities.

When we touched down at Thumrait airbase in the desert kingdom, it was obvious that things weren't going to be easy. As they lowered the ramp at the back of the aircraft, the heat of the desert hit each of us like a lead brick. 'Isn't this wonderful, Jeremy? It's nearly 50 degrees Celsius, and just look at all that sand,' were the profound words of Taff, the RAF flight sergeant in charge of unloading the aircraft. Sand was a bit of an understatement: if you like building castles on the beach, go to Thumrait and construct an entire city! There's enough sand for hundreds of thousands of castles!

Before I'd had a chance to take in my less-than-hospitable surroundings, a soldier approached me. 'Hello, Jeremy, could I ask you to go over there with the other troops and register your arrival in theatre?'

What was this? A Scottish RSM (regimental sergeant major) talking to me like a human being? This was not what I had expected: he wasn't raising his voice to me. In fact, he was being polite to everyone he spoke to, irrespective of rank or status. I picked up my kitbag and trundled across the airfield with the other troops towards the terminal building, where we registered that we had entered an Operational Theatre. This, as you might expect, is essential if the army is going to keep track of its personnel, especially in times of war.

Having registered my intention to remain in Oman for at least the night, simply because there were no return flights to the UK from Thumrait that evening, I struggled into the back of a Land Rover for the bumpy forty-five-minute ride to Camp South. As we drove along a dirt track, which the driver assured me was a main road – quite who he or the Omanis were trying to kid I wasn't sure – it struck me that this part of Oman was 'The Land That Time Forgot'. The panorama unfolding before my eyes was barren, with little going for it. The only endearing feature was the sunset, which I have to say was stunning.

Having been on the move for nigh on thirty hours, I wasn't sorry to arrive at Camp South to be met by my new boss, the regiment's commanding officer – Lieutenant-Colonel Nigel Smellie (pronounced Smiley, before you all start sniggering). The Colonel was an unassuming, jovial man who, judging by some of the badges on his uniform, had seen plenty of action, including a spot of bomb disposal. 'Jeremy, welcome to Camp South, we're delighted to have you here,' said Nigel – oops, I mean the CO. I liked him already – he hadn't raised his voice either. He introduced me to Jim.

'Nice to meet you, Jeremy,' said Jim. Corporal Reeves, who hails from Middlesbrough and is married with four kids, joined the Army at the age of sixteen, following in the footsteps of his older brother Ian. 'There's five years' difference between me and my brother, and I've always looked up to him, and that's why I followed him into the Pioneers which, no matter what anybody says, is the greatest regiment in the British Army.' It was clear that both Jim and the Colonel were passionate about the regiment, and I soon began to feel a lot more comfortable about spending the next seventy-two hours in the armed forces.

The regiment itself has a confused and somewhat disjointed history. There is mention of Pioneers as early as 1346, in the pay and muster role of the British garrison in Calais. However, the first real evidence of them comes from the year 1750, when a proposal was put forward for a 'Corps of Pioneers' with their own regimental organization. Over the centuries that followed, various records show that the Pioneers were established, disbanded, absorbed and re-created, more often than not when a messy, unpleasant or menial task needed to be done that nobody else in the Army wanted to do. The clouded history of the Pioneers clears in 1917, when at the height of the First World War the British Government decided to create a Labour Corps, who were charged with a host of duties that ranged from running the military laundry and stores to tailoring and shoemaking. I had a feeling, though, that things had changed considerably since those early days.

Colonel Smellie was determined that I should enter straight into the true spirit of the Pioneer Corps and ordered the quartermaster to issue me with all the kit I was going to need while I was at the camp. My dad would have been proud to see me standing in the middle of the desert trying on sand-coloured combat fatigues. Could it be true? Was I really about to don the clothes of a soldier and do time as a Pioneer? It was, and if I'm honest I was beginning to look forward to it.

As Jim and I walked through the moonlit camp we chatted about his home life.

'How tough is it to be away from the family for long periods of time?' I asked.

Without hesitation, Jim responded, 'It's by far the toughest part of the job, especially for Debbie and the kids. In fact, I've often said that the medals I've been awarded over the years should really have been given to my wife, who earns them every day looking after the family.'

My first real challenge as a Pioneer was to construct my own camp bed, which, I being rubbish at such things, proved more of a challenge than I could cope with after such a long journey. Come on, give me a break here, please! Have you ever tried building something under canvas in the pitch dark? Well, if you have, you'll appreciate how tricky it can be. If you're not tripping over things, you're banging your head against the poles. I was glad that the camera crew had already gone to bed, and weren't around to capture my first faltering steps as an Army Pioneer. The worrying thing about my inability to build a simple camp bed was that in the morning the commanding officer was going to expect me to perfect a number of skills associated with the construction industry. Poor man, he really had no idea what he'd let himself – or for that matter the regiment – in for.

The men of 187 Squadron were shocked to learn I was staying at the camp in a tent. For some reason they'd thought I would be staying in a swanky air-conditioned hotel back in Thumrait. No way, Jose! If I was going to do this film justice, I needed to experience Army life for real. This was, of course, my biggest mistake! Attempting to sleep when the temperature is 30 degrees C, and the wind is blowing through your accommodation at more than 35 m.p.h., is not that easy, I can assure you. And if this wasn't enough, I also had to contend with the possibility of sharing my tent with one or two of the local inhabitants! No, not the local tribesmen! The indigenous camels! But not the dromedary kind! The spider variant. Yes! And the camel spider is a less-than-friendly element of Omani life, as Jim explained: 'Watch out for the scorpions, snakes and, perhaps more important, camel spiders. A guy in another squadron had one crawl on his face during the night and it ate away a large part of his right cheek while he slept!' Great!

Although I was exhausted, there was little chance after that that I'd get any sleep. My eyes were going to be on stalks all night scanning the dark for my eight-legged enemy: they anaesthetize your flesh, then have a good old chomp while you're oblivious to their exploits.

Just as I began to drift off to sleep, overcoming my new-found arachnophobia, I was rudely disturbed by a clanging sound: 'FIRE! FIRE! FIRE! SCRAMBLE! FIRE!' It was just after five a.m. and some idiot was ringing the fire bell. Was somebody having a laugh at my expense? Did they not know I'd only been in bed a couple of hours? Of course they did! Absolutely! 'Come on, Jeremy, get yourself out of bed and report to the muster point,' barked one of the sergeants. My illusions that these Pioneers were a nice bunch had just been shattered.

Standing in the early-morning desert, feeling like death, I was informed by Major Mark Hobbs, my squadron CO, 'That fire alarm was specifically for your benefit. All newcomers to the camp need to know where to find the muster point.' I resisted the temptation to enquire why showing me the muster point couldn't have been done at a more civilized time, when perhaps I'd have managed to get at least four hours' kip! The Major continued, 'Right, now it's time for PT.'

My heart sank lower than it had ever done before during the filming of the series. PT means only one thing in Army terminology! Yes. *Physical training!* 'I'm terribly sorry, sir, but I really do think you're having a laugh now. This is a gross violation of my civil liberties. I've had no sleep and now you want me to do a rather poor impression of Sebastian Coe in this desert heat? This is outrageous!'

Very quietly, the Major, one of my many superiors, informed me, 'How do you think these men cope in the battlefield? We're infantrymen before we're anything else, and need to be at the peak of physical fitness all the time. You're definitely going to have to shape up and get on with it, Private Spake.'

I saw this as an ideal opportunity to win favour with the other eight men in my troop, to whom I had just been introduced by one of the many sergeants in the camp. Was I going to run with them all in a bid to win their respect? Not in a million years! What I did do was reason with the Major, convincing him that none of the men in 187 squadron 'really need to run. They all look as though they are at the peak of their fitness, and as for me, well, there's not a lot of hope, frankly, so if you let us off running I'll turn a blind eye to the issues of my human rights. Is that okay?'

Having narrowly escaped an early-morning sprint, the guys and I got straight on with the first task of the day. Pitching tents! Although it was almost impossible to see how far the camp stretched, because sand was being blown in my face by the now-45-m.p.h. winds, it was clear that the boys of 187 Squadron had been busy over the three months they'd been at Camp South. During that time, they had managed with the help of colleagues in other squadrons to pitch enough tents to house more than 22,000 personnel! Staggering. What we now needed to do was put up the last few for colleagues from the regiment who had been elsewhere in Oman constructing other camps in preparation for this massive British military exercise, intended among other things to remind the world that we could muster strength when the need arose.

Under normal circumstances, pitching a few tents isn't a problem, not even for me. However, no sooner had we managed to get most of the poles in place for the first tent than the canvas was being blown across the desert by the high winds, pursued by three of the lads in a bid to catch it!

Believe it or not, it took all nine of us to arrest the tent's flight and, not for the first time since the boys had been in Oman, we had to abandon construction until the wind died down. As I stood surveying the conditions at Camp South that I and my new team-mates were working and living in, it seemed to me that I was as close to hell on earth as I could get. Sand, heat, flies, dust and wind were just a few of the relentless elements these guys had to put up with every day. The showers were simply a bag of water with a tap on, which you hung above your head and washed under while standing in an open tent. And the toilets? Well, let's not go there! Suffice it to say that Deep Trench Latrine has brought a whole new meaning to toilet facilities for me. It's a six-foot deep trench over which sits a bench with toilet seats. That's the Army's idea of WC facilities in the field. Or so I thought. I couldn't bring myself to use these less-than-happy crappers in the desert, certainly not at midday when the heat and flies made this a no-go zone. When Brian, the sound recordist from my team, was caught short and forced to use the latrines, he witnessed a soldier trying to scare off a camel spider, who'd taken a fancy to his bare legs. I discovered later from one of the Ministry of Defence press corps that they had flushing toilets in Thumrait, a place I visited enthusiastically more than once during my short tour of duty. For my new Pioneer colleagues, however, this was not an option: they just had to accept that this was their lot and, like the true professionals they are, they got on with it.

By eleven a.m. on my first day in the Army, the heat was already nearing 50°C, making work impossible. I had already drunk enough water to drain a small reservoir, and was beginning to realize how a camel feels when we were stood down until three o'clock in the afternoon to rest away from the sun and sand. I should explain that six days a week the lads of the regiment start work at just after six a.m. and go on until eleven a.m., when they are forced to rest because of the heat, resuming duties at around three for a further four hours.

My enforced, and somewhat welcome, break from work gave me an ideal opportunity to find out from the lads in my troop exactly what being a Pioneer meant to them. Jim was first to answer my question: 'We are the best of the best. Some would argue that we are jack-of-all-trades and masters of none, but there isn't another regiment anywhere in the British Army that's like us. We not only build tents, fuel dumps and prisoner-of-war camps, we also carry out our infantry duties. I have done several tours of Northern Ireland, and in fact served with my brother there just before he came out of the army.'

'Did you say you'd built prisoner-of-war camps, Jim?' I asked.

'Me and some of the lads here have.'

As I chatted with Jim and the boys, I discovered that they had been one of the first units to enter Kosovo during the crisis. When they first arrived at the border, they were charged with the task of building a refugee camp, where they spent many hours looking after the now-homeless people of that troubled country, as well as entertaining hundreds of parentless children. As the march towards Pristina advanced, they were detailed off to construct a camp to hold prisoners of war. Not only did they have to build it, but they were also expected to guard it on behalf of NATO. 'This is the sort of thing, as Pioneers, we are expected to do,' continued Stuart, a lance-corporal. Indeed, as far back as 1942 the men of the Pioneers were responsible for maintaining and guarding camps for prisoners of war in Britain.

As the conversation continued, one of the lads said, 'We're considered by many other Army units to be the lowest form of life, which is so unfair. Everyone thinks we're thick because we're in the Pioneer Regiment.'

This struck me as sad: these guys work so hard, often in very difficult conditions, and yet they feel as though the rest of the Army looks down on them – including some men in the Royal Engineers, with whom they work closely. My time with them soon revealed that, despite anybody else's opinion, they are proud to be Pioneers, and so they should be! Events like D-Day, 6 June 1944, when no less than thirteen Pioneer companies were deployed on the beaches of Normandy in the first wave of troop landings, demonstrate the role Pioneers often play at the forefront of any conflict. In fact, that day, some 6,700 Pioneers landed in France, and less than a month later more than 33,500 of the regiment's troops had joined the fight to reach Berlin. Indeed, the men of 187 Squadron, with whom I was now sharing my life, had themselves been among the first troops deployed into the Middle East during the Gulf War, to say nothing of the Falklands conflict back in 1982.

While normally, as I explained, the men wouldn't be expected to return to work until three o'clock, I was summoned at two by Nigel, the Colonel. He had planned for me to do a bit of brickwork with Jimmy, another of the lads in my troop. 'How are you finding it, then, Jeremy?' the Colonel asked. Then, before I had time to reply, he said, 'We need you to help build a wall around the regiment's safe!' Trying to look neither confused nor bemused, I smiled at him and he told me where I would find Jimmy.

This is as good a place as any to explain why the safe needed to be bricked in. It houses the cash allowances for the men and, for security reasons, was being moved around the camp in the back of a Bedford truck. This was proving impractical, which was why the Colonel had decided to cement it to the ground and have it encased in a brick cage. Now, I can hear your brains ticking over: surely all that sand makes the ground incredibly soft, and therefore difficult to cement anything to?

Wrong! The ground is rock hard, and the sand full of stones, which made making cement a real challenge for

Jimmy, who is a fully qualified bricklayer. Yes! Can you imagine it? There were no supplies of the right kind of sand, and we had to use the pebble-infested muck we were standing in to make cement. Even I know, with my non-existent bricklaying skills, that the right raw materials are essential for such a job if it's going to work properly. Add to this that the bricks were concrete breeze blocks and you can begin to appreciate that things were not necessarily going to go according to plan, despite the Colonel's insistence that 'It'll be fine. Pioneers are a resourceful bunch, and versatility is their middle name, which is why the motto "Where there's a will there's a way", is apt for you right now, Jeremy!'

An hour and a half later, having sweated about ten gallons of fluid out of my system, we'd completed the task. At the Colonel's request, I autographed the top layer of cement, just to show I'd done something tangible on my first full day in the Army. Proud? Of course I was! This had been a real team effort!

Now you've probably been wondering what on earth these guys do to amuse themselves when they're not on duty. Good question! Having spent the remainder of my day helping Jim and the troop fill sandbags, I was positively bushed, and fancied a trip to the nearest cinema or a really good restaurant for a slap-up celebratory meal. Let's be honest, I'd survived one whole day in Hades and I felt like I deserved a bit of pampering. 'What are we doing tonight, then, lads?' I asked, hoping they'd already organized transport into Thumrait for us all to go and enjoy ourselves.

'There's nothing to do here, except eat dinner then write letters home, or watch videos in the mess over there,' said Stuart.

He was right: it wasn't as though they could pop to the nearest pub for a beer, or zip across town to see the latest

Hollywood blockbuster. In fact, that evening we amused ourselves with a regimental quiz night, in which the Broadcasting Barbarians Club – the name I gave to my BBC team – came a very respectable third, only hampered by a lack of sporting knowledge. Admittedly there had been an awful lot of questions concerning Russia and the former Soviet Union, which some might argue gave me and my team an unfair advantage.

My agony at having to get up at five-thirty the next morning was self-inflicted. I really should have gone to bed at a decent hour instead of standing in the moonlight, chatting with my new comrades about life in the regiment until three a.m. As I emerged from my tent into the early-morning gales, I bumped into Gaynor, who was living under canvas adjacent to me. Gaynor, a sergeant in the Royal Logistics Corps assigned to the Pioneers, was one of only a handful of women I'd encountered since arriving in the Sultanate. 'Morning, Gaynor, I hope I didn't disturb you last night when I got back. Someone had switched off the generator, and I was stumbling around like a demented chicken trying to find my tent among the sea of green canvas!'

Gaynor, who had met my team by accident when they'd walked into her tent thinking they'd found my humble quarters, was pleased to be able to catch up with me. 'Jeremy, I'm really pleased you're up. I was hoping to be able to persuade you to pose with me for a photo, which I'd like to send off to *Hello!* magazine. They often print pictures of readers with celebrities, and it would be great to have a photo of us together in our combats in the desert!'

On my first day in the Army, it had been explained to me that I should always try to keep on the good side of the company chief clerk who, in this case, was Gaynor: the chief clerk dishes out the money, etc., so I said, 'No worries. When we're on down time I'd love to oblige.'

That same afternoon at about two-thirty I stood with Gaynor while the Major caught us on film. A brief chat with her revealed that although she is a woman, 'We get treated the same nowadays in the Army. Although I have to say the blokes are great, they really look after me well. When I need a shower, for example, a couple of the lads stand on guard so that no one else comes in. It's like having loads of big brothers!'

Gaynor, like every other solider I'd met in Oman, was completely committed to Army life. Why? Well, I certainly felt an overwhelming camaraderie existed among the troops, and a sense of togetherness I hadn't experienced before. They were all determined to make the most of their lot and get down to the job, which was more than admirable, given the hideous weather conditions that prevail in Oman.

As a child, I was very excited when my parents once gave me a Tonka tipper truck and digger for my birthday. Tonka toys were mini-sized construction vehicles made of metal, and were fantastic, especially for an eight-year-old boy. I spent many a happy hour digging up my mum's plants, tipping them into my robust yellow lorry, then dumping them in the middle of the lawn. So you can appreciate that when the Major asked if I would like to help the men build a fuel dump, using a large tipper lorry and associated diggers and fork-lifts, I jumped at the chance. I was in my element, as I lifted, shifted and tipped huge quantities of sand at the back of the camp, where it had been decided that the fuel dump should be built. What struck me, as I created mayhem and confusion among my troop, was just how versatile the men had to be. Jim had been right: this Pioneer thing wasn't just about running through a field with a gun seeking out the enemy, oh no! Although, of course, they had infantry responsibilities, they also had to be able to function across a broad range of skills. I was enjoying myself so much as I charged around in the desert looking like Bob the Builder that had I been ten years younger and 100 per cent fitter, I would have considered this as a definite career option – although I'm quite certain I wouldn't have coped with doing any of these tasks under enemy fire, which the men of the Pioneers have to be able to do at the drop of a hat.

Sadly, all the fun came to an abrupt end when the major ordered us to get ready for patrolling duties. What ensued demonstrated to me the primary role of the Pioneer Regiment. I was handed my webbing and a rucksack, then ordered by Jim, 'Crouch down there, Private, and await further instructions.' As I struggled to the ground with what felt like an elephant on my back, I discovered we were about to conduct one of the regular security patrols that take place daily around the camp. We had our weapons checked by Jim and Stuart, then set off in a long snake-like line away from camp. 'What are we looking for, Jim?' I asked. I needed to know too why we'd changed roles so rapidly from building to foot patrolling.

'Jeremy, it's no good looking at me, you should be searching the horizon for potential hostility!' exclaimed Corporal Reeves. He was trying to instill in me some of the infantry skills that the men have to possess before they can even consider building a fuel dump, for example. As I got to grips with what I was looking for, I spotted something: 'Look at those footprints, Corporal. There's obviously been a few camels through here.'

Jim turned to me. 'Private, you're supposed to be looking out there across the horizon, not at your boots. Now, take yourself over there and lie down, keeping a close eye on the distance!'

We'd already walked a fair stretch, stopping every few yards to regroup, thus ensuring we were all present and correct, and now I was having to lie in the sand looking for potential enemies. I can assure you the only enemies on my mind at the time were the creepy-crawlies knocking around in the desert. Snakes, scorpions and those camel spiders all behave in a less-than-friendly manner when lain on, so I wasn't taking any chances as I got down on the ground. I asked Brian in the camera crew to keep an eye open for anything crawling up my leg. No sooner had I settled than I heard the Corporal issuing instructions: 'On the double, regroup to my mark!' Members of my troop ran towards Jim at great speed. Now, normally I wouldn't even attempt to run, but I was enjoying this Pioneer thing so much that I was determined to impress the boys by making it back to the Land Rovers, which is where they were headed.

However, as I gave chase I was ordered by Mike, the director, to ease up because of the heat. I was left, regretfully, in a cloud of dust as the men pulled away in the Land Rovers. Eventually, having thumbed a lift from a passing Army vehicle, I reached the lads from the patrol at the main entrance to Camp South, where the Corporal was debriefing them. On seeing me he immediately declared, 'Private Pile [this was my new nickname], the men and I have decided you're a crap solider! Although we have to say you did quite well with that webbing!' The lads were all having a good old laugh, thinking I hadn't worked out that they'd filled my rucksack with rocks! I hadn't mentioned the weight of my equipment at the start of the patrol because I wanted to earn some respect by doing something the others all had to do – after all, it was my job to assess how tough it was to be a Pioneer enabler. We all had a good laugh when they suggested I join the girl guides.

Okay! Why am I making such a fuss about Army life? Surely, when someone joins the armed forces they accept that life is going to be tough, and that they will often have to live in unpleasant surroundings? Well, yes, I guess you might be right. But imagine being away from home for long periods of time, and only being able to make one twenty-minute phone call a week to your loved ones. Not to mention the conditions in which you might be asked to live and work. Having spent an all-too-brief time working and living alongside the Pioneers of 187 Squadron I learnt that young men and women often enlist in the Army because there are limited career opportunities near their homes, and the Army offers everyone the chance to develop and improve themselves, with a guarantee of progression if they show commitment and dedication. There is, however, one demand made in return for these opportunities: the Army expects those young recruits to be capable of killing a fellow human being when ordered to do so, and without questioning the reasons behind it. Not only this, they also have to accept that at any moment in their career, they themselves may die in defence of the realm.

After four immensely enjoyable but tiring days at Camp South, it was time for me to pack my kit and head for home. Before leaving, the Colonel asked me to join him and the men on the makeshift parade-ground next to Regimental Headquarters. There, I was presented with the red-and-green flash of the Pioneer Regiment. Although I felt unworthy of such an honour, the gesture confirmed for me everything I'd learnt about the men, who believe in team spirit and in fulfilling the words of the regimental motto on a daily basis: 'Labor omnia vincit' translates to mean 'Work Conquers Everything' – and, boy, do those lads know how to work, regardless of the conditions!

# chapter ten
# STATELY HOME OWNER

**Salary:** Whatever is left once all the bills are paid.

**Requirements:** Applicants should possess an ancestral link with the property, be willing to let Old Uncle Tom Cobleigh and all traipse through their home and, above all, be capable of working round the clock.

**Toughness rating:** 6

I consider myself fairly intelligent and rarely find that I struggle to understand a particular situation. However, I couldn't help but wonder what planet the production team had been living on when they decided to send me to a country mansion for *Toughest Job*. What's the job? I wondered. How tough can it really be? Is it the groundsman I'm looking for, or the housekeeper, or perhaps one of the poor, downtrodden servants who spend their lives running round pandering to the lord and lady's every whim? Well, I was shocked to discover that the series producer, Juliet Rice, wanted me to follow the property's owners, Richard Gillow Reynolds and his wife Suzie, not the staff! How bizarre, I thought. I wonder why?

As I walked along the sweeping driveway towards Leighton Hall in Carnforth, Lancashire, I found it difficult to imagine what could possibly be hard about living in a huge house in such a beautiful location. What could be tough for Richard and Suzie? I hear you ask. Well, I, too, at this point was lost for an answer.

As I reached the house I spotted someone who looked like the groundsman (he reminded me of the gardener, Ted, in BBC 2's *Fast Show*). He had bright red cheeks and wore a hacking jacket with a cloth cap as he mowed the lawns directly outside the house on one of those fantastic tractor-type mowers. 'Hello, there! Nice day! I was wondering if you could help me? I'm looking for Richard, the master of the house,' I asked, above the noise of the tractor ticking over.

'Sorry, didn't catch what you were saying, young man.' The chap switched off the tractor's engine.

I had this terrible feeling that I'd just made an awful *faux pas,* but I asked him again, 'Apologies for disturbing you, but I'm looking for the master of the house. Do you know if he's around?'

Yes! I had, rather monumentally, put my size nines right in it. 'That's me. You must be Jeremy,' he said.

Ooops, I could hardly deny being Jeremy at this point, especially not with Mike and Brian beside me with the camera and sound equipment. 'Yes,' I agreed, trying not to look like a complete prat.

'Come and meet Suzie,' Richard said, in a polite but firm voice.

We stomped across the gravel forecourt towards the house in true soldier's fashion. Richard had clearly been a military man – even his wellingtons were smart! 'Hello, Jeremy, and a very warm welcome to Leighton Hall.' A middle-aged, elegant lady, who looked quite a bit younger than Richard, was standing before me. 'I'm Suzie, and it's a real pleasure to have you here, although I'm not sure what the audience will make of our problem.'

Ah, there *was* a problem, which must be the reason I'd been sent there. As she led me into the estate office for a cuppa, Suzie explained: 'The bank has given us just eight months to turn the property on its head and make a profit.'

So the production office hadn't been on another planet when they'd stumbled on the plight of my hosts.

Leighton Hall, whose history can be traced back to 1246 when Adam d'Avranches had a fortified manor constructed on the site, has had just twenty-six owners. Richard himself could trace his ancestry all the way back to Mr d'Avranches, which may explain why he exclaimed, so passionately, 'The thing is, Jeremy, my entire family's history lies here at Leighton. It's not simply a home or business, this is our heritage, and both Suzie and I want the house to be viable enough for us to be able to pass it on to our youngest daughter.'

Suzie was equally committed: 'We simply can't imagine the bank taking this place away from us, so we don't talk about it unless we have to.'

Clearly I was going to need to tread carefully around the issue that had brought me to this rather pleasant home on the edge of Lancashire.

Mike Montgomery, the film's director, had, in traditional *Toughest Job* fashion, given Suzie and Richard the run-down on my role. They in turn had lined up a long list of jobs for me to help with, which I was assured would demonstrate the efforts they were making to keep Leighton's roof above their heads. 'What's first, then?' I asked Suzie.

'You need to meet the staff who help keep the place ticking over,' she explained.

During the staff meeting, which took place at around nine a.m., I was introduced to Pam, affectionately called 'Pammy' by the lady of the house: 'She's my right-hand woman here. Without her I'd be lost.' Pam was a pleasantly warm and friendly lady, with a fantastic sense of humour, and it was immediately apparent that we were going to get on well. The rest of the team included a groundsman called Steve, who was young and looked nothing like a traditional estate gardener, leastways not in my book. In addition to his assistant, the hall employed a full-time falconer, Denise, but more about her later, as well as a host of unpaid volunteers who gave guided tours in the afternoons when the house was open to the 'GPs'. No, not a convention of doctors, which is at first what I thought Suzie meant, but the General Public.

My first challenge of the day was to assist Suzie and her team in co-ordinating a visit by a school group of about thirty kids all aged between eight and ten. Dozens of school trips turn up at the hall throughout the year to learn a little about the house's history and go on nature trails across some of the 1550 acres that the Leighton estate covers. As the double-decker coach arrived carrying the kids, I said to Suzie, 'Look, riot control is my forte! Leave this lot to me. I'll soon have them where we need them.'

Clearly Suzie had no idea of my attitude towards young people's character development, and said, 'Okay, I'm relying on you to get them to the toilets before the tour starts.'

Bless them all, they were eagerly staring out of the coach windows – and I'm a great believer in allowing children to express themselves freely . . . in other words, run amok!

Well, come on, kids are only young once, and we've all been there, haven't we? I can vividly remember some of the school trips I'd been on; normally to incredibly boring museums where you had to be frogmarched around in strait-jackets while being barked at by some dull curator. Breathing was only possible when the teachers had granted you permission. Does all this sound familiar? Well, if it does, you'll understand why I was eager for the children coming off the coach to enjoy their experience at Leighton. There was always the chance that word would spread about how fantastic it was at the hall, which would help Suzie and Richard's income, and keep their frustrated bank manager from foreclosing on them.

Because I needed to make sure all the kids went to the toilet before they wandered off around the estate, I herded them through the main gates and figured that the best way to get them to co-operate was to have a bit of a chuckle with them and allow them to run riot all over the drive. This didn't appear to amuse the adults much – Pam and Suzie were chatting with the teachers, who almost without exception were pulling faces of disbelief at me. And Suzie had obviously decided that while my technique with the children was pleasing the little ones, it was just a tad too modern in its thinking for the teachers: 'Jeremy, we'll leave Pammy to sort the children now, you've done a marvellous job. We need to head off to the cash-and-carry to get supplies for the tea shop!' That was me put in my place!

Our short trip to the local cash-and-carry in Morecambe, Carnforth's nearest major town, gave me my first real chance to talk to Suzie about the hall's problem, although the interview stopped and started every couple of minutes. Why? Well, Suzie's fairly erratic gear changes caused all sorts of problems for the cameraman – he lunged backwards and forwards at every junction and set of traffic lights, like one of those nodding dogs so popular in cars nowadays.

As I began to chat to Suzie about life at Leighton, I discovered she was a warm, kind-hearted woman who was totally committed to making the hall a success. 'Richard and I work round the clock to make the place pay. In fact Richard has put forward a number of schemes over the past five years in a bid to turn the estate into a viable business.' One such scheme, she explained, was for a number of holiday cottages to be built at the back of the house on farmland, which would then be used year-round by tourists. Sadly, a number of political factors had prevented them realizing this ambition. English Heritage, the Government's main agency responsible for protecting the best of England's legacy of historic buildings, landscapes and archaeological sites for our generation and those that follow, had expressed an interest in helping Richard and Suzie, but the assistance they could give was, sadly, limited. To all intents and purposes the pair were on their own.

Our trip round the cash-and-carry was extremely quick because the owners had refused to give the BBC permission to film on their premises. Suzie, who reminded me of Audrey fforbes Hamilton – you know, the character played by Penelope Keith in the hit BBC series of the 1980s, *To the Manor Born* – was laughing as we zoomed round the shop knocking things off the shelves on to our open-sided trolley. 'What's funny, Suzie?' I asked.

'I'm going to bring you with me more often. They're normally very unhelpful in here, but your presence has certainly attracted them to us.' It's true that being recognized by most people can have its advantages, although by the time I'd signed a dozen or so autographs Suzie was getting impatient. 'Come on, Jeremy, we need to get these ice-creams back to the house.'

Enough said. I scurried behind her with the trolley and loaded the car for the return journey. The cameraman elected to sit in the front passenger seat this time. 'Jeremy, I need to capture some reverse shots of Suzie and a few of your POVs.'

POV stands for Point of View. Let me explain: often when you are watching a programme that involves people travelling in vehicles, you will see shots of the street and roads while the driver or passenger is talking. These shots are put in the can to enable the film's editor to have some flexibility when mixing shots. It's called Point of View because the shots are meant to represent the scene that someone would be seeing from the front passenger seat of a car, etc. Does that make sense?

Back at Leighton we off-loaded our booty at the tea room, which is situated on the lower ground floor beneath the music room, then caught up with Pam, who had dished out duties to the small band of volunteers ready to face the daily onslaught of GPs. The gates to the estate open for them year round at two o'clock after the school groups have left. 'What's my job, then, Suzie?' I asked, wanting to be as much help as possible.

Suzie, having seen my performance earlier in the day with the school group, decided, 'You can be my assistant this afternoon during the tours. We've got some influential ladies' groups from Morecambe booked on the afternoon-tea tour of the house, and we want to lavish attention on them.' Clearly, buttering up the public had become an evil necessity for my host, who nevertheless seemed to enjoy having thousands of strangers in the house every year. However, having to follow hot on her heels throughout the tour didn't sound as if it would be as much fun as I'd had with the kids, although I am, of course, capable of causing chaos with any and all. Then Suzie said, with an almost pathetically desperate look on her face, 'Jeremy, once the tour is over I want you to manage the plant shop. The first group we have are from a gardening club, and will probably want to buy plants. I'm relying on your salesmanship this afternoon to help us earn some additional cash.'

You're probably wondering now why Suzie and Richard hadn't turned their house into a wildlife or theme park, like Woburn Abbey or Beaulieu. Well, the simple answer to that, I guess, is their location. The house, which is nowhere near as big as a place like Chatsworth, is situated on the edge of the Lancashire/Cumbria border and is relatively remote. Hotels and guesthouses are limited, which means that the area couldn't cope with the Mongol hordes arriving in droves at Leighton. Anyway, I'm not entirely sure that they would want to convert their front lawn, which stretched for nigh on half a mile up an undulating slope, into a home for roller-coasters. *I* wouldn't want to destroy such a beautiful scene. The schemes they have in place, such as the house tours, tea-shop, plant sales, school trips, garden tours and falconry seem to work well. In addition to the daily routine, the house also plays host to a number of corporate and specialist public events each year, including a 'Proms in the Park', where the public sit on the lawn in front of the house with their picnics, singing 'Land of Hope and Glory'.

Anyway, enough of all that. The tour of the house revealed that people could walk the length and breadth of the property, sitting on the furniture, lifting the porcelain and generally asking silly questions, which, if they'd been listening to the tour guide in the first place, they wouldn't have needed to ask. 'What's going on here, then, Suzie? Normally, stately homes have the family's accommodation blocked off from the public,' I said.

'Not here at Leighton,' she replied. 'We like people to come and sense the entire house, which is why we let them sit on the furniture and such like.'

My only concern at this point was to keep a close eye on the visitors and make sure they didn't break anything as they hurled themselves into the chairs like small children on the rampage and, yes, I would know all about that, thank you very much!

The tour lasted just over forty-five minutes, and then the group headed off for their cream teas while I got to grips with the plant stock in the greenhouse at the side of the property. I know diddly squat about plants and gardening! I couldn't tell the difference between a hyacinth and a hydrangea. What sales technique was I going to use if I couldn't impress the gardeners with my extensive green-fingers knowledge? Simple! I'd use just one sales technique: ENTRAPMENT. Yes, I intended to fill the greenhouse with as many of the wonderfully cheerful tour guests as I could, lock the door and refuse to let them out until they parted with their cash and walked off with as much stock as they could carry.

Did it work? You're not kidding! They were all laughing at my jokes and hadn't even noticed the door being locked as I thrust plant after plant into their hands, telling them how wonderfully they would grow in their gardens.

While all of this was going on, the camera crew were busy filming Suzie at the back of the house talking to people about *her* garden, which is rather stunning – and the public are encouraged to walk all over the grass! Leighton is a true revelation in terms of a visit to a stately home.

My sales trick worked wonderfully – until Susie and the crew tried to get into the greenhouse. Ooops, tumbled! 'Sorry, Susie, this door seems a bit sticky to me,' was my rather pathetic excuse for trapping the gardeners in my glass cell as I unlocked it.

'What's going on? Don't these people want to watch the falconry?' Susie asked. As I explained that I had already sold over a hundred pounds' worth of plants, which wasn't bad given that most of them were selling for around two pounds, she immediately shut the door and helped me pack them into bags. But she'd shut the door so fast that the camera crew found themselves locked out! I had redeemed myself: I'd demonstrated that with a little bit of cheek you could achieve results. That afternoon proved to be Susie's most successful plant sale ever.

Afterwards I showed the group, who were all clutching their plants, to the front of the house to watch the falconry display. Denise was standing on the lower lawn with Gorbachev in her hand. Oh, it was a wonderful sight! 'Mikhail Sergeiovich . . . no, *slushinka* . . . *davai* . . .' Please, friend, come on, get on with it. No, I've not gone mad, this was me trying to help Denise get Gorbachev, a Russian steppes eagle, to fly for the assembled crowds. Leighton is home to a small but impressive collection of birds of prey, and Denise is the resident expert, who gives demonstrations twice a day. That afternoon Gorbachev became my best friend as he flew up on to the roof of the house and refused, in typical Soviet style, to surrender to the bourgeoisie below by flying around and giving a demonstration of his hunting skills.

Finally, at five p.m., I managed to catch up with Richard, who was busy in the dining room cleaning the silver, and learnt some more about the history of Leighton. He spoke of his forebear Richard Gillow, who in 1822 was the first of Leighton's owners to take a modern approach to the hall: he had commissioned a new façade, which forms the backbone of today's neo-Gothic structure. A Victorian extension was added to the side of the house in 1870, by Richard Gillow's son – Richard Thomas Gillow. I'm sorry, folks, is this beginning to sound like I've forgotten everyone's name, and that I've chosen 'Richard' to represent anyone who has had the pleasure of owning this troubled hall? Well, before you accuse me of going mad, I can assure you that all of these people did exist, and that, like the current master of the house, they were all called Richard. That said, the current Richard explained, 'Because the finances were getting tight a few years ago, we had to convert the Victorian wing into flats.'

So not only were they having to let the public wander through the house to earn a few bob, they had also been forced to convert a large chunk of it into flats for strangers to live in. It was clear that my hosts were determined to take whatever steps were necessary to keep their ancestral home, no matter how it affected their own personal lives and space. I'm not sure many of us would want the world and his dog dragging through our living rooms, prodding and poking at the furniture, would we? Still, they appeared to have little choice.

'Come on, boys, that silver's been polished to death. We need your help to move the furniture.' Suzie had joined us.

'Dare I ask what furniture needs moving?' I asked.

'Tonight we have a function in the house, and need to shift the furniture round to get tables in to accommodate eighty or so dinner guests,' replied Suzie matter-of-factly.

Let's face it, it's quite normal to let eighty of the great unwashed into your front room for dinner, isn't it? Apparently if you live at Leighton Hall it's an almost nightly occurrence. Suzie, seeing my bemusement, went on, 'It's another way of earning a few quid to keep the bankers happy. We convert four of the main rooms into dining accommodation. The caterer has arrived and is in the kitchen preparing tonight's food, and the client will be here by seven, so we need to pull our fingers out and get on with it.'

By this time the entire team of staff had arrived to help shift furniture around the rooms and wheel in the chairs and tables needed for the diners. There was even a band setting up in the music room.

'It's all in a day's work,' Pam assured me, as I gave myself a hernia lifting six chairs at once. Now, Pam ought to know –

after all, she's been with the Gillow Reynoldses for a long time and had nothing but pleasant things to say about them. 'They're an amazingly dedicated couple, and care passionately about the hall. While Suzie looks after the house and its associated activities, Richard manages the farmland and estate grounds. It would be a huge shame for them to fail.' It was clear to me that Pam wasn't saying this simply because the BBC were filming her but because she was committed to her employers and the house as well. This is something that had struck me about everyone who worked and lived at the property: they treated it as if it lived and breathed with them. This may seem like a lot of old hogwash, but it's true: to them the house was like a much-loved pet.

Rearranging the Gillow Reynoldses' home took just over an hour, by which time we were all flagging. Suzie, whose day normally starts at seven a.m. in the office, had rushed upstairs to get changed before the chairman of the local Law Society arrived. No, she wasn't in trouble: the local branch of the Law Society were that evening's clients. 'Will they behave, do you think, Suzie? I mean, we've left the family silver out.'

No sooner had I finished asking her this cheeky question than she whisked me off to the front door to meet the first of the evening's guests, who was indeed the chairman. Suzie and I lavished love and affection on each and every new arrival.

Where was Richard while all this was going on? A good question. 'Suzie, where's Richard at the moment?'

'He'll be squashed in the office, surrounded by the excess furniture, dealing with the accounts for today,' she replied.

She wasn't kidding: I found him huddled in a corner up to his ears in furniture trying desperately to count the day's takings, while the band in the next room struck up.

When the last guest left Leighton at one-thirty, I said farewell to an exhausted Suzie and Richard, who spend seven days a week, eighteen hours a day, worrying about the estate. They've tried to develop a hundred and one different ways to earn the money that the bank so desperately wants to see. They suffer a complete lack of privacy, having to keep the doors to their home perpetually open to the public. Many people would argue that it's difficult to keep their businesses afloat, and I'm sure they'd be right, but for Suzie and Richard this isn't simply a business: it's their home and heritage all rolled into one. Their ancestral history creates emotional baggage and that's impossible for them to ignore. Their life is tough in a way that not many of us could appreciate. After all, most of us believe that people who live in big houses and talk eloquently couldn't possibly find life difficult. In the case of the Gillow Reynoldses I would beg to differ.

# chapter eleven
# RAPID RESPONSE PARAMEDIC

*Salary:* £16,000–21,000 per annum

*Requirements:* Applicants must be capable of working under often stressful conditions, independently of supervision. They must be level-headed, caring and compassionate.

*Toughness rating:* 12

It is rare, as you will probably have noticed from reading this book, for me to be excited about the prospect of carrying out an assignment in search of the nation's Toughest Job. However, I was over the moon to hear that I would be joining the Rapid Response Paramedics team, of the Greater Manchester Ambulance Service. Why was I suddenly looking forward to a particular film? Come on, let's face it, it had to happen, didn't it? There had to be one job that I'd be delighted to investigate further on behalf of the people of our green and pleasant land. But why the role of a paramedic?

Well, when I first appeared on BBC One in *Airport*, one of the charities I chose to work with was the Air Ambulance service across the country, which you may be amazed to learn is funded entirely by you, the people, and not the government. I have spent many a spare hour organizing fundraising events, signing autographs, shaking buckets, giving after-dinner speeches and generally making a nuisance of myself in helping to keep the life-saving helicopters in the air over Cornwall, East Anglia, Essex, Lincolnshire and Wales, not to mention the North-West and North-East. As a result of my work with them all, I have developed an immense admiration for every one of Britain's paramedics, whether they are flying around the country or travelling along its roads providing emergency care to us all. How tough was I going to find it all? I thought I knew – but did I?

My instructions, as always, were simple: make my way to Belle Vue ambulance station in Manchester and seek out Phil Howcroft, a paramedic officer who was married with two children, and one of the people in charge of the newly established Rapid Response team.

When I arrived at Belle Vue, which was not only Phil's base but also housed the Greater Manchester Ambulance Service's control room – you know what I mean, the room where all the 999 calls are handled and from which the vehicles are despatched to assist – I found Phil cleaning an Astra estate car with PARAMEDIC written all over it. 'Nice to meet you, Phil, and I'm really looking forward to this. But before we start, can you tell me where your ambulance is, so I can dump my gear?'

Phil, who immediately struck me as someone I would enjoy working with on account of his cheerful disposition, looked at me as though I'd taken leave of my senses. 'This is it,

Jeremy!' He was pointing at the now gleaming Vauxhall Astra.

I should explain before we get too engrossed in the job itself exactly what Rapid Response is. Rapid Response teams have sprung up all over the country as a direct result of government service standards. The government, via its Department of Health Ambulance Consultative Committee, ruled that all ambulance services across the country should have a trained paramedic on the scene of an emergency within just eight minutes for at least 75 per cent of all 999 calls. Have you tried traversing a busy town or city in the rush-hour? Eight minutes, believe me, isn't a great deal of time in which to do it, but ambulance services had to find a way of reaching the target while maintaining the highest standards of patient care. Hence Phil's Astra estate: a car or motorbike can travel at much higher speeds than a conventional ambulance, making its response more rapid. These vehicles are normally manned by one paramedic, and are not intended to convey a patient to hospital, merely to deliver urgent care to them while an ambulance makes its way to the scene of an incident to transfer them to the nearest Accident and Emergency department.

Phil is one of nearly 1500 staff who work for the Greater Manchester Ambulance Service (GMAS), which provides emergency ambulance coverage across an area of more than five hundred square miles to a population of nigh on three million people. The staff work from thirty-five ambulance stations around the Greater Manchester area, and last year alone the service took 272,000 999 calls, responding to 235,000 incidents, as well as carrying out 802,000 non-emergency patient journeys. In addition to its core emergency service, the GMAS operates a fleet of non-urgent Patient Transport Service vehicles, which are used to ferry members of the public to hospitals for outpatient appointments. They also operate an NHS Direct call centre, which provides twenty-four-hour health advice and information to the general public, often directing callers to the most appropriate form of medical assistance.

'Right, then, Phil, where do we start?' I asked, eager to get on with the job in hand.

'Well, we'll relocate from Belle Vue to Hope Hospital, which is one of our standby locations, and then I'll show you some of the equipment in the car, which I will be relying on you to pass to me when I ask for it,' responded Phil.

Paramedic Phil had been with the ambulance service in Manchester for about twenty years. 'My dad died of a heart-attack when I was young, and I stood by completely helpless. From that moment on I decided I wanted to be a Paramedic so that I could at least try to assist people to survive similar situations,' he explained. The first few moments of our conversation revealed just how dedicated Phil was to his more than worthwhile job. He'd joined the service as a cadet at the age of sixteen, then worked his way through the ranks to his current role.

Phil showed me the various bags of equipment we had with us, which included an automatic defibrillator – the gadget you see in programmes like *Casualty* when they electrically shock a patient's heart back into action. I was praying we weren't going to need any of this stuff over the next few days, but had a feeling it would all be coming out of the car at least once. As you know, I need to get as involved as possible with each job, but clearly, I thought, this was going to be one of those professions where I was going to be taking a bit of a back seat. How wrong I was. Although I couldn't render medical care beyond basic first-aid skills, Phil felt I should be as involved as possible, which is why he said next, 'Just grab the pager there, Jeremy. I'd like you to look after the communications and liaise with Hazel in the control room, as well as do all the essential navigation.' This was beginning to sound like an awful lot of work for one mere mortal like my good self.

No sooner had Phil passed me the tiny black pager than, in true *Toughest Job* style, it started warbling like a canary. Before my very eyes flashed a host of codes, which meant absolutely nothing to me. 'Phil, it's a Delta Zero—' I hadn't even finished reading out the information on the pager before another computerized gadget started bleeping at me.

'Don't worry, that's a tracking system, which not only enables Hazel to get an accurate fix on our location but helps her decide if we are the best-placed vehicle to head to an incident. It gives us the same information as the pager,' said Phil calmly. 'Have you got those map co-ordinates sorted out yet?' he asked. By now he had pulled away from the hospital and switched on the car's blue lights and sirens.

'Yeah, down to the traffic lights then left, left, left,' came my less than confident response. You may be wondering why I was repeating myself. Well, I know from experience that when you are being guided by a navigator it is much better, as a driver, to be told the all-important direction you are heading more than once, as this eliminates the possibility of any errors. Fortunately for me, Phil is also a qualified driving instructor and has taught a number of paramedics to drive. The map references had come straight out of an Ordnance Survey map, so almost any fool could work out where they were going – including me!

Driving through the centre of Manchester at speeds in excess of 70 m.p.h. with lights flashing and sirens blaring gives you an adrenaline rush. However, there is a huge responsibility on the drivers' shoulders to ensure that every action they take doesn't endanger other people's lives. To say you need eyes in your backside is no understatement. As we sped towards numerous sets of traffic lights I was learning quickly to scan constantly for pedestrians, cyclists and other motor vehicles. Above the noise of the sirens, I said, 'Clear, clear, clear,' which told Phil that a particular junction was clear of any hazards on my side of the car.

In addition to my observational role, Phil had put me in charge of changing the siren sound from a wail to a yelp. Does this sound like I've gone mad? I haven't, honest! As I quickly discovered, people tend to drive around Britain's roads with their eyes closed, often failing to notice huge great big blue flashing lights in their rear-view mirror. The siren has varying tones to alert these wonderful people, as well as anyone else in the street, that you are behind them and in a hurry to get to an emergency. Not that it was doing us much good with one particular driver, who pulled out right in front of us. As you know, I'm normally very calm, but I couldn't resist a little yell out of the window: 'Look, you idiot, that's what the sirens are for! Get out of the way!' A rather embarrassed driver quickly pulled up on to the kerb to enable us to pass.

'That's typical, to be honest. People don't look in their mirrors enough.' No sooner had he said this than we were confronted by a learner driver trying to overtake a car that had pulled over to let us get past! I won't repeat what advice I offered the learner, I'll leave it to your imagination, but suffice it to say that the version transmitted in the programme was much more polite. The show does go out before the nine p.m. watershed, you know!

While all this excitement was going on, the pager and in-car tracking system continued to bleep, giving us information about incidents all over the Greater Manchester area. Things in the car certainly seemed crazy to me. It was proving increasingly difficult to keep concentrating with all the noise around me. What did occur to me while I was grappling with the maps and giving Phil his directions was just how tricky all of this must be when you're in the vehicle on your own. Let's face it, Phil and his colleagues have to drive the vehicle at speed, navigate, operate the information systems *and* control the sirens. And all of this before they've rendered any sort of medical assistance to a patient. If all this sounds like information overload to you, it's just possible that you're not cut out to be a paramedic, and shouldn't be considering a career change.

Modern paramedics are confronted by masses of equipment that they need to know how to operate. Their role is a far cry from that of their colleagues in the nineteenth century. The original ambulances were horse-drawn and first introduced in the 1850s during the Crimean War in support of Florence Nightingale and her nurses. After the signing of the Geneva Convention in 1864, ambulances and their occupants, both wounded and able-bodied, have been considered neutral on the field of battle. The first recorded motorized ambulance of the United States took to the road in 1916. It operated in Mexico during America's push against the revolutionary general Pancho Villa, although quite how busy its crew was kept is not known.

When we arrived at the first incident of the day, within five minutes of the call coming through to us, I grabbed the kit Phil needed and we rushed towards a first-floor flat in a warden-patrolled old people's home. An elderly lady was having difficulty breathing. 'Hi, my name's Phil and I'm a paramedic. What's your name, love?' Phil was kind and gentle as he ascertained the patient's condition. 'Could you pass me the oxygen cylinder from that bag there, please, Jeremy?' he asked, then continued to chat with the patient, trying to help her relax so that her breathing would ease.

As Phil treated the patient with oxygen and fluids, it became clear to me that the traditional role of an ambulance operative to transport a patient to hospital had changed for ever. Paramedics now need to have an intimate knowledge of an enormous range of medical conditions, and how best to treat them in the first instance.

After we had handed over the now slightly recovered lady to the crew of a conventional ambulance, so that she could be taken to hospital, I took the opportunity to find out more about the training. Phil explained, 'When you first join the service there is an eight-week classroom training course, then twelve months of supervised on-the-road training. After passing this element you are classified as an ambulance technician, which allows you to offer limited primary care to a patient. It's only after a further twelve months on the road as a technician that you can apply for training as a paramedic.' When qualified, paramedics have to undergo regular checks to ensure that they are still capable of doing the job, which is a bit like commercial airplane pilots, who are assessed every six months to check their competency. By the way, I discovered later that the lady we had just treated was comfortable and doing well in hospital.

Our next call was a bit vague. Hazel explained on the phone, 'You're looking for a middle-aged man under the influence of alcohol, who is reported to be lying unconscious in the street. The police are on their way to the scene, Jeremy. Can you let Phil know, please?' Ever aware of my role in the car, I immediately informed my paramedic guide and mentor. 'Phil, the police have been called to this next job. I'm not sure I like the sound of that. Is it normal?'

'To be honest, Jeremy, we often attend jobs with the police. There are some quite dangerous areas around here, especially at night, and we need to make sure we don't expose ourselves unnecessarily to danger. Drug and alcohol incidents in certain areas of Manchester can prove pretty hazardous.' As we passed through yet another red traffic light, with extreme caution of course, I had to ask, 'Have you ever been involved in any situations that posed a threat to your own life?' This seemed like a particularly important question given that Phil and the other Rapid Response paramedics work alone, and not in twos like the paramedics who man the ambulances.

There was a slight pause: Phil was scanning the road to make sure that I was still giving him accurate information about safety issues while we travelled at high speed. 'There was one incident, which occurred ironically when I was working on a two-person vehicle. My partner and I had been called to a house where it was reported a man had collapsed in a similar fashion to the call we're now heading for. When we reached the house a young, fairly fit-looking guy answered the door and said a patient was lying unconscious in the living room. This all seemed quite routine to my colleague and me, so we went on in. Much to our surprise we didn't find anyone unconscious there. We turned round and were met by the guy who had been at the front door but who was now wielding a large machete and screaming, "I'm going to kill you both, you pigs!"'

'Charming! What happened next?' I asked, as I continued to track our progress towards the current incident on the map, praying that this job wasn't going to involve any threat to our personal well-being.

'Well, we sat on the living-room floor for more than forty-five minutes being threatened by this man. Fortunately I had a radio in my pocket and was able to open the channel to the control room, who alerted the police. Eventually the man, who had recently been released from a psychiatric ward, gave himself up to them and we left the house unhurt.' This, according to Phil, is 'all in a day's work'. He and his colleagues often face the threat of physical violence from patients who are either drunk or disturbed in some way. Paramedics are only trying to help people: why should they have to put up with this type of abuse, irrespective of a patient's condition?

As we approached the incident I switched off the siren. I could see no sign of any collapsed persons, just lots of really young kids hanging around a policewoman's car, looking on with mischief in their eyes. 'That's strange, Phil, the policewoman seems to be on her own. Do you reckon this is a bit of a hoax?' I asked.

What possesses people to waste the time of the emergency services is a bit beyond me, I must confess. But, then again, when you have people calling 999 because their hairdryer no longer works, what can you expect? Seriously, no word of a lie: I was sitting in the control room of another ambulance service recently when a woman phoned wanting an ambulance crew to come and repair her blessed hairdryer! What is the world coming to?

Anyway, back to the story of our collapsed patient. We discovered from the policewoman that there had indeed been a drunken male on the ground, who was by no means unconscious as he picked himself up and ran when he saw the police car approaching. 'Phil, what do we do in such situations? If a concerned member of the public has called because they are worried about this drunk chap, should we not try to find him in case he really is hurt?' Yes, I know, I sometimes ask questions that seem a little bit illogical – after all, if this chap has run off, what chance is there of us finding him in a place as big as Manchester?

Much to my surprise, Phil responded: 'As we head off, we'll certainly have a scout around just in case he's collapsed out of sight not far from here.' After thirty minutes we couldn't find any trace of our mystery man, so I contacted Hazel to notify her that Phil and I were now clear for the next job.

We'd been on the go for six hours without any real break, but fortunately hadn't had to deal with any major incidents. Most of the calls we'd received were to attend to people suffering from shortness of breath. This seemingly common condition had accounted for more than two hundred of the 360-odd 999 calls that the Manchester ambulance service had received thus far that day. In addition to helping a lady whose chip pan had caught fire, causing her to inhale the smoke fumes, we answered a call to a distressed mother, who had discovered that her infant son had a rash on his back, and an extremely high temperature. Phil calmed not only the baby but also the distraught mum. Within just ten minutes of our arrival on the scene, the baby was being transferred by ambulance to the nearest A and E department, where it was discovered that he had a mild infection.

As we left, I had an opportunity to chat with some of the onlookers who, like all human beings, had become curious about what was happening at number fifteen! I explained to two pensioners at the front door of number thirteen why the paramedics were there, and what I was doing with them. Then I asked, 'Do you think you would like to do this job?'

Without hesitation, one responded, 'No, no, no, no, not really. They're bloody marvellous them para-what's-a-names, though, ain't they?' I wasn't going to argue. Phil and people like him really are incredible, but why do they do this job? It's relentless, and you never know from one incident to the next exactly what will happen or, for that matter, what you are going to face when you get there. Is it the salary and working conditions that keep paramedics coming back for more? No, I don't think so. It seems to me that this is a calling, an overwhelming passion to help others.

Just as I thought I was about to get a bit of a break from the stress of having to navigate, communicate and generally provide assistance, the bleep did what it does best and warbled again, rendering my now rumbling stomach deprived of sustenance. 'Where are we off to, then, Jeremy?' Phil asked, in his usual calm but jolly manner. As I read the location and job details to him, we sped off across the city towards one of the many smaller towns that surround Manchester.

As we turned into a street lined with terraced houses, which reminded me a bit of *Coronation Street*, we could see a gaggle of people standing in the middle of the road waving frantically at us. A sixteen-year-old girl was lying dazed on the pavement. According to one onlooker, she had been delivering free newspapers and suddenly fallen to the ground.

As Phil took the usual crucial information from the patient, I was asked to fill out the incident-report paperwork. Every ambulance service in Britain requires its paramedics and technicians to complete an incident report detailing each patient's personal details, condition and any treatment provided to them. These forms are essential for a number of reasons, not least having an accurate record of a particular incident in case the patient, sadly, passes away.

Before I'd had a chance to finish noting the girl's address, a conventional ambulance arrived to transfer the patient to hospital. As Phil and his two colleagues carefully slid the girl, who was now wearing a neck brace, on to a hard board intended to protect her in case of spinal injury, I had the perfect opportunity to chat with the other paramedics about the job. I discovered that one of the crew members, Angela, was Phil's wife. They had met while he was still a cadet trainee some eighteen years earlier. 'I caught sight of her at one of the training sessions and thought she looked pretty fit, so I offered her a lift home, saying I lived nearby. The fact is, I lived at completely the opposite end of the city, but she was worth it!' Phil told me.

'You must both find it difficult to switch off at night when you get home. How do you cope with the job?' I asked, wanting to know just how tough things can be when you're both married to the job as well as each other. Angela had decided she didn't fancy being on national television without any make-up, so she declined to comment, leaving Phil to talk to me, as she and her colleague took the patient to hospital. (The girl was treated for concussion, then discharged.)

Phil and I started to pack away the equipment as he tried to explain how difficult things can be for him and his wife. 'Obviously some days are extremely tough, especially when you have had to deal with a child's death, for example, but because we are both paramedics we can be a great comfort to one another. Major incidents, where a number of people die, can really knock you for six, but between us we sort the emotions out. It's like falling off a bike. You just have to get right back on again and keep going.'

Not long after a short but well-earned coffee break back at base, we found ourselves charging to a bank on the outskirts of the city centre, where it had been reported that an eighty-two-year-old male had collapsed and was unconscious. We battled our way through the usual hordes of stupid drivers and went straight in to the bank with all the equipment. What greeted us was the sight of an elderly gentleman who had been lying spreadeagled on the floor for more than ten minutes without breathing. Now, this was something I'd witnessed at Heathrow Airport on a number of occasions, but it was still traumatizing. But I had to get down to the job, putting aside the obvious emotions that such an incident provokes.

Phil was already clearing the patient's airway as he asked me to assist him to give CPR, which I had been trained to do when working at Heathrow. (In an emergency, rapid response paramedics will call on members of the public to help give CPR, but only if they are fully trained in CPR.) CPR, for those of you unfamiliar with the term, means cardiopulmonary resuscitation, and is used to restore the heartbeat in a patient whose heart has arrested. It combines the techniques of artificial respiration with the application of external heart massage to keep blood flowing through the patient's body.

It was obvious that Phil needed to work fast if there was to be any hope of helping this poor man. As we continued to give chest compressions to try to force blood to flow into the heart, two more paramedics joined us, which gave me a chance to get some vital information from the bank's staff about the patient, such as his name and address. Phil and the boys struggled for twenty minutes to try and resuscitate him, but sadly he never regained consciousness.

This was the most graphic demonstration I had seen of just how tough being a paramedic really is. Often, despite their best endeavours to save a life, they fail, and have to come to terms with this quickly before they are called to the next incident where their help is needed.

In my book, paramedics deserve the applause of us all for doing such a worthwhile job. Although, thankfully, I hadn't had to witness any major road-traffic accidents, or large-scale incidents involving hundreds of people, I had gained a vivid impression of a paramedic's life during the twelve hours I had spent on the road with Phil. Was it tough? For sure! Especially when you consider everything a paramedic has to be able to do. Would I want to do the job myself? Without doubt! It's incredibly rewarding: even though some patients may die, many more do not, and every call is worth attending.

# chapter twelve
# INDUSTRIAL FORGE WORKER

**Salary:** Paid by the piece, so dependent on output.

**Requirements:** Anyone suffering from shyness when intensive hard physical labour is mentioned need not apply. The position requires team players, with a good sense of humour. Applicants should be used to working in temperatures in excess of 120°C, and, above all, have cast-iron hearing!

**Toughness rating: 13**

Just by way of a change, I stood in Birmingham outside the house of Dennis Sanders, safe in the knowledge that I knew exactly what I was letting myself in for – or so I thought! I'd been told that I would be working at Morgan Platts, one of a handful of industrial forges still left in

Britain. Like the fool I am, I had managed to convince myself it was going to be a bit like working in my local blacksmith's forge, where they make the odd horseshoe now and then. This couldn't have been further from the truth.

'Hi, Dennis, I'm Jeremy! It's great to meet you,' I declared. Dennis is married with two teenage daughters, and has the firmest handshake I have ever encountered in my life. In fact, he nearly crushes your hand when he says hello.

I walked into his kitchen nursing my semi-battered digits to meet the family.

'Sue, look who's here!' said Dennis, and introduced me to his wife.

'So, Dennis, describe your job to me,' seemed like the perfect way for me to bring the nature of Dennis's chosen career to our audience.

Although I knew what sort of work I would be sampling with Dennis in my quest for Britain's Toughest Job, I hadn't appreciated the conditions in which he and his colleagues worked.

'We get in to work at about five-thirty a.m. and start up the furnaces. Once they're hot enough, we load in the day's first lot of steel bars. You'll soon find it hard to breathe, as the temperature in the furnaces reaches about 1250°C!'

Was Dennis trying to put me off, or was he simply trying to make his job look tougher than anybody else's? Good question! Can you imagine what 1250°C feels like? It's about five conventional electric ovens all set to 250°C standing next to each other with the doors open, chucking out heat. Pretty warm. 'Dennis, you're having a laugh! It's not that bad, surely?' I was praying and hoping that my new friend with the Agrippa handshake had been kidding.

Sue couldn't resist the opportunity to respond on Dennis's behalf: 'I've never actually been to the forge, but the pictures I've seen would put anyone off,' she said.

This was going to be the only opportunity I would get to chat to her about Dennis, so I asked her, 'What sort of state is he in when he gets home?'

'Completely exhausted, which is no good if there are jobs that need doing around the house. He'll sit down in the living room with a cup of tea when he gets in and within five minutes he's fast asleep! The job really takes it out of him.'

'Surely he could find an easier way to earn a living?'

'He loves the job – in fact, he's obsessed with hammer number five, which is the one he works on five days a week. Sometimes I feel like second best when he talks about that blessed hammer. I'm sure he's more in love with that lump of metal than he is with me! I've tried to convince him to look for some other kind of work, but it's the forge and hammer number five for him every time!' Sue had clearly resigned herself to Dennis's passion.

'I'll see you in the morning at about five-fifteen,' said Dennis, with a knowing smile . . .

Next morning I stood nervously in Dennis's office.

'Jeremy, the first and most important thing to do is kit you out with your safety clothing,' he said, still smiling.

Naturally, I began to worry about the level of danger I might be facing as I put on my protective steel-toe-capped boots, Perspex goggles, disposable ear-plugs, ear-defenders, leather apron and leather spats – which would protect my legs from molten metal flying through the air!

It was clear within minutes of starting work with Dennis that this was going to be one of the most dangerous environments I had been asked to work in for the series. 'Now's a good time to quit if you want to, Jeremy,' said my new boss, and went on to explain how difficult it was to get staff to work on the hammers, which I could hear in the distance, pounding their first steel bars of the day. 'Young men come and go here like the wind, to be honest. Most people don't want to earn a living like this. It's hot, dirty and hard. The majority of the men here have worked on the hammers for more than ten years. In fact, there's only one lad who's under thirty, and although he's not been here long he's a really good worker. He often confesses, though, that he wouldn't be here if he had a chance to escape.'

Escape wasn't an option for yours truly, so I responded, 'Quit? Oh, no, in for a penny in for a pound, me. What is it they say, "*Nil desperandum* – onwards and ever upwards"?'

Resplendent in my brand-new work overalls and looking like something from a science-fiction movie in all my safety gear, I walked with Dennis across the somewhat ramshackle forge compound to the building that housed the company's main group of hammers. It is almost impossible to describe the conditions that exist inside the forge. As I entered the area around hammer number five for the first time, I was shocked by what I saw, and amazed that men still worked in such an environment to earn a few quid. What was it like? *Victorian!* No word of a lie – it reminded me of the images I'd seen of the Industrial Revolution of Victorian Britain.

Let me expand on this. Picture a dimly lit warehouse-sized shed with a corrugated roof in which stand six or seven heavy industrial casting hammers. Each hammer pounds away from six a.m. until nine-thirty p.m., and is manned by two shifts of workers. Alongside the hammers is a line of furnaces, in which the average temperature is 1250°C. The furnaces spit out flames as steel bars are loaded through open doors to be heated up ready for forging into shape under the mighty weight of the closest hammer. As I knelt towards the furnace to get a feel for what it was going to be like during the day, I could hardly believe the heat – I'd never experienced anything like it.

Having to shout above the incessant thud of the hammers, I ventured to offer my first impressions to John the cameraman, who was already dripping with perspiration and struggling to work in the intense conditions: 'THIS IS TRULY UNBELIEVABLE! I'M HAVING TROUBLE BREATHING ALREADY AND I'VE ONLY BEEN IN HERE FOR A FEW MINUTES. I'M NOT SURE I'M GOING TO LAST THE SHIFT.'

By the way, if you're wondering what the hammer looks like, it's about thirty feet high and ten feet wide, shaped a bit like a large church bell with a hole in the middle. Through the centre, attached to a long shaft, is the hammer head, or punch, as some might call it, which pounds down on to a die fixed into the base of the hammer. It's surrounded by cables and wires, which lead to a group of foot pedals, from where the hammer is operated by the men.

'Jeremy . . . co . . . e a . . . d m . . . e . . . t the l . . . a . . . s.'

'DENNIS, IT'S NO USE, I'M NOT TOO GOOD AT LIP-READING, MATE! I CAN'T HEAR A DAMN THING YOU'RE SAYING. YOU'LL HAVE TO SHOUT A BIT LOUDER!' I removed the earplug from my left ear and gestured towards it.

'JEREMY, COME OUT HERE TO MEET THE LADS!'

Although I'd only been inside the shed for about five minutes I was over the moon to be going outside for a breather.

'Jeremy, I'd like to introduce you to the other men you'll be working with today.'

Before Dennis had a chance to perform his introductions, John was yelling: 'Stop! I've got a few problems here with the camera, Jeremy. It's going to need to reacclimatize a bit.' The move from the extreme heat of the shed into the cooler open air had affected the camera and its lens, and both items of equipment needed to cool down before we could resume filming. At times like this, believe it or not, I have to stand and wait in silence. It's almost impossible for me not to talk, so it's a real challenge to keep quiet. Why did I have to refrain from chatting? Well, when you are filming something that is based heavily around actuality, a television term for real-life, it's important that you capture as many first-time reactions from people as possible. Then you won't need to ask the contributors to say or do something again, which may make them feel uncomfortable and cause the film to look less than natural. Nicky, who was directing, was eager for us to capture the first introductions on tape as they would definitely be used in the series, thus I had to keep silent.

During the ten minutes that I waited for the camera to acclimatize to the outside world, the men went back into the shed to continue the relentless task of forging metal – they are paid by the number of items they forge, and not by the hour, so they can't really afford to spend more than ten minutes away from the hammer before it starts to affect their earnings. That's tough! I later discovered that the piece-payment system was a great incentive for Dennis and the lads to work as a team, although in this day and age it seems a bit draconian to me.

My enforced silence away from the men gave me time to reflect on the overall conditions that surrounded me. Although I've never experienced a war, and hope I never will, I couldn't help but wonder whether the constant thud of the hammer and shuddering of the ground caused by the pounding of metal was a little bit like the feeling you experience during an air raid. Frankly, it was a chilling thought that sent shivers down my spine as I was shaken like a cocktail by the trembling earth beneath my feet.

Having loaded the furnaces with more steel, the boys came back outside so that Dennis could rattle off the all-important introductions. 'Jeremy's here for the day, boys, to give us a hand,' said Dennis, who was trying to encourage them to be as media-friendly as possible. 'We need to show him as much about the job as we can without endangering his life.' My immediate reaction to this went something like,

'Dennis, did you say *endanger*? Hello, I'm not planning to get close enough to anything to endanger my life. Thanks very much!'

The entire team responded in unison: 'Yeahhhh . . . like, we think not! We're going to let you get right in there for a real taste of the job!'

'Marvellous, great, smashing and lovely. Thanks, boys, I'm so glad you've heeded the words of Nicky about making me suffer a little!' I said, in a less than cheery *Toughest Job* voice.

Dennis interrupted me: 'Right, then, those bars are going to be useless unless we get going, so I'd like to finish introducing you to the lads.' I listened intently and shook hands with the team, which included Dave and Chris. I'd be working closely with them over the next eight-hour shift.

The boys immediately struck me as a great bunch who enjoyed a laugh despite their working environment. 'Are you ready for this, then, Jeremy?' asked Chris, with a wry smile on his sooty face. 'We need to go and put some more bars in the fire. It may sound easy but we'll see how you go.'

The team of six men, including Dennis, were now having a right old laugh at my expense. Then again, this is pretty much the format for the series, so I ignored them and went straight back into that living hell!

The ambient temperature inside the shed had now reached 115˚C, and the closer I got to the furnaces the more unbearable the heat became. Clutching a pair of long-handled tongs I picked up the first steel bar. 'BLIMEY! THIS THING WEIGHS A TON, THIS IS MADNESS!' I shouted at Chris, who was gesturing at me to get a move on. 'HOW MUCH DOES THIS LITTLE BLIGHTER WEIGH, ANYWAY?' Chris held up a whole stack of fingers, which were difficult to see through my steamed-up glasses. I later discovered that each bar I was loading weighed in at ten kilograms – that's half the average packed suitcase to you and me. I managed to load about twenty bars before fatigue started to set in. I know – this all sounds a bit weedy, doesn't it? Like I'm wimping out in the first ten minutes of real hard graft! OK, maybe it does, but have you ever tried lifting ten kilos of steel with a thin pair of long-handled tongs, while battling against flames and a temperature in excess of 1200°C? No? Well, I can assure you it's not easy. You see, you can't hold the tongs close to the tip near the steel bar because you're going to burn your arms on the furnace wall, aren't you? After just a few bars you begin to tire, and the heat burning your face makes it almost impossible to breathe. There's absolutely no fresh air, and you're gasping as you battle to keep up with the pace of your colleagues. The heat and flames were beginning to make me feel like Red Adair – you know who I mean, the chap who goes round the world putting out oil-well fires. Sadly, putting out the furnace fire raging in front of me was not an option until nine-thirty p.m., which seemed like a lifetime away to little old chubby me!

For health and safety reasons I needed to take breaks every ten minutes, and decided to drag a few of the guys out with me. This would give me the ideal opportunity to chat with them about working on the nightmare-inspiring hammer number five. 'Lads, this really is tough! I cannot get over the conditions inside the shed. How on earth do you motivate yourselves to get out of bed in the mornings? This place will probably haunt me for days and I've barely started working!'

They had seen people come and go before, and had a chuckle to themselves about the work as Dave explained, 'I've worked in a forge since the age of fifteen, and wouldn't know what else to do. The conditions are rough but I've got a mortgage and a family to look after, so I don't have a choice.' The lads all nodded in agreement.

Then Chris chipped in, 'When you need to feed your family you find the energy to get out of bed, no matter what faces you. Work is pretty hard to find around here nowadays. This whole area of the Midlands was once dedicated to forging, and most people worked in the industry. Because of the cheaper steel production in Eastern Europe and the Far East most of the forges have closed, so you have to be grateful for what work you can get, despite the bloody awful conditions that exist.'

The Black Country and the West Midlands became synonymous with industrial forging during the Industrial Revolution in the nineteenth century. People like Isambard Kingdom Brunel catapulted the country into the modern era using iron and steel. The expansion and development of a railway network across Britain, as a result of Stephenson's invention of the *Rocket*, created an urgent need for forges to churn out large castings of wheels and axles. There was an enormous demand for people to work in newly created forges across the Midlands, and virtually the entire economy of the region was driven by steel production. Today, because of cheap imports from around the globe, as Chris had said, almost all of the forges have closed. The handful that haven't, like Morgan Platts, face bankruptcy on a daily basis. In fact, the lads of hammer number five were working under constant threat of redundancy, as a group of financial administrators struggled to salvage the business from collapse. Perhaps this was why they didn't complain too much.

After just ten minutes, Chris said, 'Come on, then, Jeremy. Dennis wants to get you pounding a few bars now in the hammer.'

Sure enough, there was Dennis standing alongside number five with a beaming smile, clutching a steel bar. 'RIGHT, WATCH THIS CAREFULLY. YOU NEED TO PLACE THE STEEL BAR IN HERE. USING THIS PEDAL, LET THE

HAMMER DROP DOWN AND THEN ROLL THE BAR ROUND TO FLATTEN IT DOWN A BIT . . . LIKE SO. ONCE YOU'VE GOT THE BAR LIKE THIS, YOU NEED TO PLACE IT ON TO THE TOP OF THE DIE HEAD, THEN PUSH THIS PEDAL. WATCH CAREFULLY!' As Dennis stepped on the pedals, I witnessed the huge hammer head thunder down from a great height and crush the bar as though it were a piece of dough. Seconds later we'd produced components for Vauxhall car engines. 'DO YOU WANT TO HAVE A GO AT THE FIRST STAGE THEN, JEREMY?' enquired Dennis.

'I'LL HAVE A GO, BUT I CAN'T PROMISE NOT TO MAKE A RIGHT BALLS-UP OF IT ALL.' I was terrified at the thought of injuring not only myself but Dennis.

As I gingerly put pressure on the first pedal, there was a mighty expulsion of hot air as the hammer pounded towards my little pair of tongs like a bullet train racing across Japan. The power of this beast was awesome, and it caused me to rebound away from the pedals as it pounded down. Fortunately, I managed to keep my footing, and finished the first stage of the job.

However, Dennis could see that to allow me to progress to placing the steel into the die head might be a big mistake. Each die is a precision-tooled instrument, and the last thing he wanted was for some great fat oaf from the BBC to cripple the day's production. 'JEREMY, WE'LL TAKE YOU OVER THERE TO ONE OF THE SMALLER HAMMERS FOR SOME MORE TRAINING BEFORE WE GET CARRIED AWAY HERE. THE LAST THING WE WANT IS FOR PRODUCTION TO HALT BECAUSE YOU'VE BROKEN THE DIE!'

Phew! A lucky escape! Dennis was letting me off the hook. A very wise move.

As I headed for one of the smaller hammers where more delicate engine components were being cast, I persuaded

Dennis to pop back into the fresh air for a breather with me and the crew. Collectively we managed to consume what seemed like a gallon of water, as we stood trying to regain a near normal pace of breathing. 'John, would you want to work in there permanently?' I asked the cameraman. I wanted to know if I was the only person not enjoying the experience.

'No way! It can only be described as horrendous! But if I had no choice I'd probably have to.'

John had hit it on the head, if you'll pardon the pun! Most of the men didn't have a choice, and just went through the motions, relying on each other to get them through the day. Dennis, however, enjoyed his work: 'It's lovely. Every time that hammer slams down we are producing something concrete. I can walk away from here every day knowing that thousands of useful items have been made that most people take for granted. That number five is an impressive piece of machinery, it's beautiful, and it's a real pleasure working with her. The boys all think I'm a bit mad, but I love this job.'

While I really liked Dennis, I was beginning to feel his colleagues might be right – maybe he was a little bit crazy. 'Dennis, how on earth can you like it in there? Never mind the heat and the noise, it's so dangerous. You need to be some sort of masochist to enjoy it!'

Dennis chuckled. 'You're right, it can be a bit dangerous. Once I was working with my brother in another forge when he hit the pedal with my hand under the edge of the hammer. The next thing I knew I was lying in hospital having lost the end of a finger. Despite that, though, I love earning a living doing this, and wouldn't want to be anywhere else doing any other kind of job. It's lovely men's work!' I couldn't understand how he could be so passionate about it, but it takes all sorts in this world, and I wasn't going to argue with him.

Back in the forge, Dennis and Chris wanted to demon-strate to my team and me just how hot the steel bars get. 'JEREMY, COME OVER HERE WITH JOHN!' yelled Dennis, who was clutching a small foil-wrapped parcel.

As John and I headed across the inferno-like shed, we caught a glimpse of Chris pulling a steel bar out of the furnace with his tongs. As we reached him we could see that he'd laid a couple of slices of bread and cheese on top of a metal cupboard. 'WATCH THIS, JEREMY, IT'S BETTER THAN A MICROWAVE,' Chris shouted. He wafted the steel bar over the bread and within a second he had cheese on toast! Yes! I did say *one second*!

Then Dennis unwrapped his foil parcel to reveal the ingredients of an all-day English breakfast. Within seconds he'd made himself a four-slice toasted sandwich. The only thing that worried me about this ultra-fast cooking method was that the boys were eating their handiwork with the blackest hands you've ever seen. Still, I guess if you always cook your lunch in such conditions a bit of dirt on your hands won't upset your stomach, will it? I was left to thank Natalie for organizing a bite to eat for us in the conference room at the other side of the company's premises, where I could scrub the filth off my hands.

Fortunately, the steel being used in the smaller hammer was much thinner and lighter, which meant I was able to get up a bit of speed once Dennis had shown me how it was done. 'ARE YOU HAPPY WITH THAT, THEN, JEREMY?' he enquired. I gave him a thumbs-up and set about the tasks of pounding, casting and cutting rods of metal into car compo-nents. Although the steel was lighter, the job was, neverthe-less, back-breaking. None of the machines is height-adjustable, so you spend most of your time stooping towards them to get the task done. You can't sit down, and to compound the problem, you have to move back and forth

from the furnaces collecting rods, which in itself is exhausting because of the tremendous heat. I was tiring again after
just twenty minutes, and completely forgot that I was standing less than a foot away from the furnace with my back
facing this torrid heat. Then, 'JEEPERS! MY BUM'S ON
FIRE!' I shrieked.

The boys looked on, laughing. 'DON'T GET TOO CLOSE
TO THAT FURNACE, JEREMY. YOU'LL BURN YOURSELF!'
observed Dennis, who was fighting back the tears of laughter.

'DENNIS, HOW MANY OF THESE WOULD I NEED TO
PRODUCE IN AN HOUR, AND HOW MUCH WOULD I GET
PAID?' This seemed the perfect question to ask my cheerful
boss, especially as this is a piece-rate job and I wanted to be
able to afford a few beers after I'd finished work.

Dennis thought for a moment. 'WELL, JEREMY. YOU'LL
NEED TO KNOCK OUT SOMEWHERE IN THE REGION OF
650 PIECES AN HOUR TO GET JUST SLIGHTLY MORE
THAN THE MINIMUM WAGE. IF YOU HAD A BIT MORE
EXPERIENCE YOU'D EARN A FRACTION MORE PER HOUR
ON THIS PARTICULAR HAMMER. THE BOYS ON NUMBER
FIVE WOULD EARN SOMEWHERE IN THE REGION OF
SEVEN OR EIGHT POUNDS AN HOUR.'

My face said it all. I was flabbergasted to think I would
need to produce somewhere in the region of 5200 steel
components to earn just thirty-four pounds in a day, and
that's before the taxman has had his share. It was now obvious why the men didn't take real breaks for lunch or tea, and
why they rely so heavily on each other to earn a living. After
all, if you had a few slowcoaches on the team like me, you
certainly wouldn't be earning much.

My day continued apace with more pounding, shifting,
cutting and loading. I never ventured back towards the
dreaded number five hammer, preferring instead to keep
nipping into the less fume-filled air outside the shed, where

I had at least a fighting chance of being able to breathe. I stood in the doorway watching Dennis's team working, and was amazed at the pace they managed to sustain. They were churning out more than a thousand heavy components an hour, which in those conditions is nothing less than a miracle. I thought at the time that the Queen ought to introduce a medal for those working in the face of industrial adversity. Each and every one of the blokes at Morgan Platts were worthy recipients of it, even though it wouldn't be much of a reward for the type of work they do.

Although there isn't much for the lads to laugh about at work, I gave them a good chuckle as we cleaned ourselves up after our shift. 'Here, this doesn't seem to lather up very much, this soap, does it?' I asked as I tried to wash the soot off my face.

After several minutes of side-splitting laughter Dennis shouted, 'That's a grease block, Jeremy! You'll find the soap, which lathers beautifully, in the other container over there.'

Great! Even a simple task like washing my face was beyond me, but then again I was so completely knackered I didn't have the energy to care, or even offer the lads a clever retort.

After a day like that there was only one place to head: 'Come on, lads, let's get ourselves to the nearest public house so that I can buy you all a beer. You've certainly earned one.'

Sitting in the pub was the last opportunity I had to chat with the men about their lives, and what drove them to work in such archaic conditions. 'Well, lads, I have to say you're welcome to the job! I've no desire to swap places with you. In fact, if I could drag you all away from here, I would.'

Dennis, Chris, Dave and their colleagues all looked at me, knowing they would have to turn up at five-thirty the next day and continue the struggle to make ends meet. Dave said, 'Jeremy, until you arrived here I'd never really thought much about the job and its conditions. I have to say you've opened my eyes up to it all, but you've also made me a bit depressed. It really is a tough way to earn money. Thanks, Jeremy.'

My heart sank. I've always feared making people feel inadequate or trapped in their jobs when we've been filming, and for the first time ever I'd managed it.

Dave continued, 'Don't get me wrong, Jeremy, it's been great having you here and I'm grateful to you for making me realize what the forge is really like. Never having worked in any other environment, I'd always considered it to be normal, but clearly it's not everyone's idea of normality.' Thankfully he had understood that I'd made my comments out of concern for this great bunch of blokes all getting on with it. In fact, I defy anyone not to have admiration for people like him and the other boys who work in our ailing forging industry. Although I didn't enjoy the job one little bit, the friendly banter among the team of hammer number five made me see just how lucky I was to be able to walk away from it all.

Next time you get into your car, spare a thought for men like Dennis and the team who slog their guts out five days a week in the noise, dust, dirt and heat, casting parts to make it go along. Would you want to swap places with them? I would dare to suggest probably *not*!

# conclusion

**F**or those of you who were paying attention at the beginning of the book, you'll remember that my quest to find the 'Toughest Job in Britain' has been a bit of a competition. Each and every one of the truly amazing people who have participated in the series has been vying not only for the title, but also the prize that accompanies such a worthy accolade!

Trying to decide who should win, and more importantly *why* they should win, has been the single toughest thing I have had to do for the series. After all, how do you decide what is tough? Is it the rate of pay, or perhaps the mental stress that makes a job tough? Is it hard physical labour, or the general working conditions? Shane Woollas demonstrated how earning a few bob as a journeyman boxer can be physically tough, and so did Dennis Sanders, in the industrial forge in the West Midlands. His working conditions almost defied description!

The £6.43 I earned for two seventeen-hour days as a farmhand with Nick and Kyra Somerfield in Bethlehem, Wales, certainly proved that the rate of pay can be an important factor when trying to decide which of the jobs we'd covered was toughest. Then, to make things even more tricky, there was Suzie Gillow Reynolds who, with her husband Richard, faced the daily challenge of trying to keep their ancestral home from being taken away from them by the bank. The mental stress that this charming pair faced would have made many a good man give up long before!

Maggie Barton showed me how to deal with working for an almost tyrannical boss, never mind that it was her husband Roger. This dynamic pair are surrounded by tons of dead fish six days a week, not most people's idea of the perfect job. And speaking of perfect jobs, having teenage revellers chuck up all over me every day wasn't the easiest task I've ever faced, although with the guidance and boundless energy of the effervescent Paul Mobbs, holiday rep *extraordinaire*, I was able to leave Tenerife without a huge dry-cleaning bill.

Sadly I can't say the same for my exploits with Dave Hulme in Blackpool. Swinging from left to right on a piece of twine, with the remarkable Dave at my side, some 480-odd feet above Britian's best-known seaside town did leave me with brown underpants – which reminds me of the fun-packed days I spent with Julie and Tex at the circus, learning how to be at the sharp end of a knife-throwing act. Although I'm not necessarily in a hurry to repeat the experience, I learnt from Julie and Tex that some careers are more a way of life and a passion than simply a job – despite the money. When I think about unpleasant jobs, I couldn't fail to mention Kenny Young and his incredible colleagues, who battle against a tide of effluent every day to keep our sewers clear of debris.

The quirky aspect of gainful employment saw me standing less than forty miles from my home in Essex clutching a rubber tube, frantically trying to remember when to suck and when to blow. Although you could not fail to like Paul Kelly and his staff, inseminating his turkeys will remain an image in my nightmares for many years to come.

One job that contrasted with almost all the others was Phil Howcroft's: paramedics really are very special people, who constantly strive to maintain the health and quality of life of their patients, often in the face of danger, stress and chaos.

As I sat in my office contemplating all of the above, it became increasingly difficult to reach a final conclusion. Frankly, every single person who agreed to let me into their lives to scrutinize their jobs is a winner in my book, if you'll pardon the pun. There can be no doubt that, during my search, I've come across, and had the privilege of working with, some of Britain's hardest grafters. Many do jobs that the majority of us wouldn't even consider. I cannot therefore stress enough how hard it has been to select the one job that, above all others, is the winner of the title.

In the end, and after much deliberation on my part, it was a close-run thing, with Phil Howcroft, the rapid response paramedic from Manchester, coming third with a score of 12. In second place was Dennis Sanders, a most worthy contender, who scored 13. So who won, and what was their prize? Well, this is normally the point in any competition when the drums start to roll and you sit waiting eagerly for someone to open a gold envelope with the all-important winner's name inside. But, because this is a book, I can't create a lingering drumroll. You'll just have to use your imagination, and visualize the tension that exists at such events.

Taking into consideration the danger element of all the jobs I covered, I drew the conclusion that being a 'builder for the battlefield' involved a whole range of dangers, not least, of course, the possibility of having to work under enemy fire. In addition to this, the levels of stress under which the Army Pioneers found themselves on a daily basis was hard to match. Have you ever spent long periods of time away from your family, trapped in one of the bleakest places in the world? Finally, as I thought about the living conditions that prevailed for the men of 187 Squadron, 23 Pioneer Regiment, I couldn't get the images of the deep trench latrines out of my head, or that every meal was shared with thousands of flies, or that sand constantly blew in your face because of the 45-m.p.h. winds!

Given all of this, and despite so many worthy contenders, I decided that Jim Reeves and his colleagues in Oman simply had to win. In my humble opinion there can be no doubt that these men really did have it 'Toughest' this time round!

When the production team and I thought about the prize we could award the lads from 187 Squadron, we could think of nothing they'd like more than to come back to Britain for a few days R'n'R (Rest and Relaxation). This would give them a chance to see their loved ones, and have a break from the relentless conditions they would ordinarily have had to endure for over six months, until early December. Jim and the lads had no idea what we were up to – or, for that matter, that we'd arranged for their families to be waiting at RAF Brize Norton for their Boeing C17 aircraft to arrive direct from Thumrait airbase. As the men emerged from the aircraft, I informed them, 'Boys, there's no doubt, you do have the "Toughest Job in Britain" of this series.' The sight of the men being reunited with their families for the first time in three months was emotional, to say the least. In fact, three of the production team were crying more than the relatives! Bless them! To make the day extra special we'd arranged for everyone to have a slap-up meal and a night's sleep in a nearby luxury hotel. I won't go into detail about what happened when we arrived at this true oasis for the men. Suffice it to say that we awoke the next day feeling very much the worse for wear.

Having read this book some of you will be thinking, 'Hmmm, maybe my job's not as bad as I thought. Perhaps I shouldn't grumble about the pay, conditions or the boss.' How many of you would want to swap places with Kenny Young and his sewer-flushing colleagues? Or have knives thrown at you twice a day, like circus performer Julie Bradley, who earns around £70 per week. Probably none of you, if the truth be known! But then again, no doubt some of you out there are now thinking, 'Who is Jeremy trying to kid? These jobs aren't tough! Mine's harder than that by miles.'

Beware! You never know, I may just knock on your door one day and ask you to prove to the nation that you've got it toughest! In reality my search has only just begun!